CASE STUDIES

IN FESTIVAL AND EVENT MARKETING

AND CULTURAL TOURISM

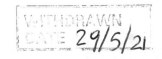
Edited by
Jane Ali-Knight
Donna Chambers

LSA

LSA Publication No. 92

Case Studies in Festival and Event Marketing and Cultural Tourism

First published in 2006 by
Leisure Studies Association
The Chelsea School
University of Brighton
Eastbourne BN20 7SP (UK)

A catalogue record for this book
is available from the British Library.

ISBN:
1 905369 03 4
978 1 905369 03 4

Cover design, layout and typesetting by Myrene L. McFee

Cover images provided by Dreamstime.com
Photographer credits where known: Dragon boat rowers, Nicholas Rjabow;
Rock concert, Kutt Niinepuu; Baloon festival, Steven Brandt

Printed and bound by CPI Antony Rowe, Eastbourne

Contents

CASE STUDIES IN FESTIVAL AND EVENT MARKETING AND CULTURAL TOURISM: AN INTRODUCTION

Donna Chambers and Jane Ali-Knight

Centre for Festival and Event Management
Napier University Business School, Edinburgh, Scotland

This collection of papers emanates from the 2005 Leisure Studies Association Conference hosted by the Centre for Festival and Event Management at Napier University, Edinburgh. For the conference organisers, the focus on 'Festivals and Events: Beyond Economic Impacts' was inspired by a joint Tourism Society Scotland/LSA seminar — 'Running Events in Scotland: Local, National and International Perspectives' — held in Edinburgh in March 2003. This seminar highlighted the growing interest in, and lack of awareness of, the measurement of impacting factors with regards to the expanding festival and event industry. Several of the speakers from public bodies such as Edinburgh City Council and the Scottish Executive emphasised the need to expand current festival and event analysis beyond economic impacts with a strong desire to attempt to measure the social and cultural impacts of events — particularly on host destinations.

The LSA 2005 conference featured more than 80 papers from a very diverse and international range of writers and researchers. This text pulls together an eclectic mix of some of the case studies presented, revealing a strong focus on festival and event marketing and cultural tourism. It offers a balanced selection of interesting festival and event case studies from academics and practitioners alike from around the globe, and that is where its interest and relevance lies.

Impact and importance of festivals

Nowhere is the impact of festivals and events more evident than in Edinburgh (UK). Steve Cardownie (2001), Festivals Champion for the city, emphasises this when he says that "Edinburgh's Festivals are a vital part of city life — both for local residents and for the hundreds of visitors who come to Edinburgh each year." A recent economic impact study by key stakeholders in the city outlined that the Summer Festivals generated around £127m of new expenditure into the Edinburgh economy, £31m of income and an additional 2,500 full-time equivalent jobs which would not have existed if the festivals did not take place (City of Edinburgh Council, 2005). The multiplier effect on tourism businesses in the city is also significant with hotel occupancy rates typically soaring to 80–90% in the capital during the festival period. Edinburgh City Council claim to be making £150million yearly from the festivals, making Edinburgh one of the fastest growing cities in the UK (*The Guardian*, 2002). The study also stresses that economic impacts is only one of many factors in the success of a festival, and one of the key strengths of the festivals is their ability to position Edinburgh as a 'Festival City' and maintain this in the face of increasing competition from other festivals. The Edinburgh Festival Community recognise the competitive nature of the industry and have commissioned a report, aptly entitled 'Thundering Hooves', to examine this in further depth and ensure that Edinburgh stays ahead of the field. While every festival must have identified cultural outcomes and associated criteria, some will offer only marginal economic benefit and others may have less obvious social impact (Graham Devlin and Associates, 2001) It is therefore unrealistic to measure each festival against the same criteria but to recognise the growing economic, social and cultural importance of festivals and events.

The case studies presented in this volume complement work that has been done in the area of economic impacts of festival andevents(Hall, 1992; Allen et al., 2005) and also give insight into the social and cultural impacts of events. All events can be seen to have a direct social and cultural impact on their participants and this impact can vary from a pure entertainment or aesthetic experience to increased civic pride, community cohesion and cultural expansion (Allen *et al.*, 2005). Events can also help to politicise communities and bring key issues to the forefront to debate, uniting communities under a common goal or cause. The following case studies address some of these issues and give an insight into the wider contextualisation and benefits of festivals and events.

Festival and event marketing

Much has been written on the ability of festivals and events to market a destination, position them in the marketplace and help create a desirable image to key market segments. In both theory and current applied activity, destination marketing is seen to assist a city in designated goals of tourism development, while also complementing the aims of the holistic strategic plan of the place. The core drivers of any strategic plan are to raise the competitiveness of a city and attract internal investment and improve the image of the destination, while also ensuring the best possible environment for citizens of the destination (Ali-Knight and Robertson, 2003).

The use of image as a strategic destination management tool, and the measurability of its effects, has been common in the destination management literature. However, what has been clear is that current research has not developed one clear conceptual framework for this evaluation. Cities, enthusiastically, aim to market themselves and develop a destination image through the use of festivals and events as a key component in their tourism portfolio.

This process of 'imagineering' a destination is not always advantageous: it can often serve to polarise economic and geographic disadvantage and alienate the host community (Robertson and Guerrier, 1998). The risk for many cities is that attempting to compete in the international festival and event arena, the cost required to compete at this level — and with short-term economic benefits unlikely and image-change being a long procedure — leads to a lack of focus for the destination, displaced funding and no clear image narrative (Ali-Knight and Robertson, 2003). What is clear therefore is that festival and events *do* have a place in destination marketing and image generation, but that this process must be carefully planned, researched and monitored and there must be a clear 'fit' with the strategic plan of the destination.

Cultural tourism

Cultural tourism is seen to attract many definitions, as outlined in Buczkowska's chapter in this text, but it is evident that it can be seen as both a product and a process. Festivals and events can provide a key cultural product that can serve as a pull factor to the destination. Festivals and events are also part of the cultural process and policy of the destination, for example as outlined in Edinburgh's Cultural Policy which states that 'Culture is the mechanism through which individuals, communities and nations define themselves' (City of Edinburgh Council, 1999). It is this role therefore of festivals and events in helping to preserve, authenticate and develop the cultural framework of a destination that is explored in this text.

The chapters

In Chapter 1, Mark Stewart, Tourism Development Manager of Liverpool Culture Company, examines whether Edinburgh's festival and events meet the needs of target tourism markets. Written whilst Mark was an employee in the Economic Development Unit at Edinburgh City Council, the chapter examines the role that festivals and events play as part of a product portfolio of a destination matched against the needs of an identified tourism market. He analyses the role of festival and events in meeting the needs of Edinburgh's target tourism markets — UK short breaks, European City Breaks and International Association conferences. Edinburgh's strategic approach to festival and event tourism is compared with another destination — Melbourne, chosen because of the perceived similarities as both cities strive to maintain their competitive edge through the development of a successful, focused and well-known festival and event portfolio. Key findings indicated that festivals and events are being used to increase visitor numbers to Edinburgh and that there is a strong link between the market for festivals and events and tourism generally, showing that they are meeting consumer needs. However, he further argues that when it comes to using festival and events strategically to reposition Edinburgh to different markets, conclusions are less easy to draw. What is clear however is that festivals and events are an increasingly important product and positioning tool for destinations and that this is evident in Edinburgh. Finally, Stewart offers practical recommendations for future research in this area including conducting research with visitors to Edinburgh, devising festival and event marketing imagery for all key stakeholders to include on marketing communications to target markets, and carrying out benchmarking with other cities — this is being conducted, as noted earlier, with the forthcoming 'Thundering Hooves' report.

The theme of event marketing and destination image is explored further in Chapter 2. Ferrari and Adamo's case study focuses on a small Italian town, Rocella Ionica, where an annual International Jazz Festival takes place. They too examine the use of destination image as a flexible marketing tool and its ability to help position a place as a desirable target destination for specific target consumer groups. They devise a model to illustrate the main effects of an event and to show their relation to tangible effects such as an increase in tourist flows and new investment, as well as intangible effects related to place awareness and destination image. They attempt to define and describe the relationship between the place image and the event: in the case study this involved investigating the image of Rocella and the impact of the event on the town from the residents' point of view. Results revealed that the festival was successful in repositioning Rocella from a traditional seaside resort to a vibrant festival town appealing to new, younger, more diverse target markets. Finally, they analyse how the festival aids image improvement and increased notoriety of the destination and — through the festival's success, particularly in attracting the mass media — how the perception of the destination is changing.

Chapter 3 moves to another part of Europe, Portugal, and away from analysing festivals and events in the context of destination image to an examination of the Mateus Palace Music Festival (MPMF) as a critique of performing arts marketing. Rodrigues and Correia identify the changes impacting on the performing arts sector, resulting in the need to adopt a more strategic marketing approach. Application of marketing to the performing arts sector is explored and the marketing strategies used by MPMF are examined. They discuss the 'negative predisposition' of many performing arts organisations when it comes to the marketing of their festival and events and the inherent clash with the creative value of the organisation. Performing Arts marketing is evaluated in the context of the marketing mix and its relevance and benefit as a management tool is emphasised. The marketing strategy of the Mateus Palace Foundation (MDF) is evaluated within the context of declining audiences, funding shortages and increased competition. Traditional marketing theory: target market analysis, the marketing mix and product positioning strategy are applied to the MDMF. Findings reveal a tight fit with these traditional strategies and the 'serious' music festival as outlined in the MDMF. If it is to survive into the future then an understanding of its market and the need for a pro-active marketing strategy enforcing the need to attract external funding and consolidate its own revenues is necessitated. The case study reveals an apparent awakening by the MDMF to the need to reverse current marketing practice and extend it to include market research and planning. The chapter therefore serves as a useful blueprint to other performing arts festivals, illuminating the importance of effective marketing to their future development and success.

Chapter 4 moves away from traditional marketing approaches and Europe to examine the Dragon Boat Race Festival (DBRF) in China. Moreira uses the festival to discuss the evolution of festivals and events rooted in traditional culture against the backdrop of emerging destination development. Culture as a motivating factor to visit a destination is discussed as well as ideas of authentic, indigenous culture as a competitive tool for destinations. Issues such as loss of authenticity and the commodification of culture, due to increased demand, are examined. The Dragon Boat Race Festival, as the most prestigious Chinese festival in Western Countries, is presented as a case study illuminating the contribution of Chinese culture to the world. The DBRF can be viewed as both a sports and cultural event and is therefore successful in attracting visitors with motivations in each of these areas. The DBRF is intriguing as it introduces the debate of how to balance the significant economic yield of a festival with preservation of cultural integrity. Moreira shows that culture and economy are not necessarily incompatible and can be mutually beneficial. Culture can be seen to have an economic value that can be used to preserve and enhance it rather than destroy it. The case study stresses the cultural authenticity of the DBRF and how as part of a portfolio of festivals and events it can contribute significantly to the competitiveness of the destination.

Chapter 5 continues the theme of cultural and event tourism with Buckzowska's evaluation of Poznan's International Fairs. She describes how the Fairs had cultural significance as a way of offering a 'window to the world' for the city during communist times also offering otherwise limited contact with foreigners. The Fairs were very much seen as an embodiment of Polish, and the city's, cultural life. The concept of 'Trade Fair Tourism' is discussed and its development and contribution to 'real' cultural and event tourism is outlined. The cultural legacy of Poznan, in terms of music, song and dance, is represented in the variety of events that the city holds. Experimental contemporary events as well as events that popularise historical traditions of the city are also discussed. Poznan is reviewed against various definitions of cultural tourism and the economic and social regeneration of the city is emphasised. Cultural events are seen to shape the city's value, character and inhabitants. The importance of the interaction between the myriad of events and the tourist infrastructure within the city is discussed. Thus the case study provides a useful insight into cultural transformation and regeneration through event tourism.

In Chapter 6, Long and Sun's paper brings us back to the UK, to the North West of England, and evaluates the role of Chinese New Year festivals in helping to recreate Chinese Culture in the UK. They discuss the development of 'Chinatowns' in York, Manchester and Sheffield as places for holding Chinese themed festival and events. The festivals are discussed in the context of 'diasporic' community festivals and their contribution to "social inclusivity, place promotion, identity building and inter-cultural communication" (p. 107). The concept of diaspora is seen to be a useful tool for the analysis of festivals and cultural events originating from ethnic communities, and is significant due to the dispersed and diversified nature of the UK Chinese community. The growth of Chinatowns in UK cities is charted and their role as representing symbols of belonging and identity, structures, ownership and power within the Chinese community is discussed. The growth of Chinese New Year festivals is also seen to be symbolic of the linkage with other communities as they become spectacles for non Chinese communities and tourist attractions in their own right. The case study cities reflect the growing desire and recognition of the power of China as an economic and political force and the desire to do business with fast growing Chinese outbound markets. The staging of Chinese community festivals in British cities is therefore seen to be a significant driver in increasing 'cultural business diplomacy' with China. Thus the festivals are seen as a vehicle for developing relationships between, and within, local Chinese communities.

In the final chapter Finkel offers a case in which the relationship between festival, identity and place is examined in the context of a Contemporary Arts Festival. The role of community arts festivals in providing a collective emphasis for the local community and engendering their pride and support is explored. The focus of the paper is the Lafrowda Community Festival in St Just and its reliance on local community support for its continued existence. The study is interesting and relevant as it introduces problems and challenges associated with broader contemporary festival funding and support for small community festivals that are seen to fall outside government cultural funding agendas and private sponsorship ideals. Contemporary cultural policies and political agendas are explored and the move to comply with governmental economic and political motivations for festivals is critiqued. In particular, the view of festivals as panaceas to help achieve social inclusion and community cohesion is discussed. Finkel stresses the need for a further examination of the role of community arts festivals in the UK in the light of this changing governmental cultural agenda. In the example of the Lafrowda Festival she finds that arts festivals can make a major social contribution to an area, enhancing community life and making St Just a 'better place to live'. The chapter ends, significantly, arguing for a more holistic approach to festival funding and support that does not focus purely on economic and political motives but recognises the inherent value of the community arts festival in widening access to and involvement in the arts, engendering a sense of community pride and a 'feel good factor' that remains within the local community once festival time is over.

Conclusion

We hope that this volume will help stimulate discussion about the true value and benefits of festivals and events to public bodies, private organisations and ultimately to the communities and destinations that host them. The case study approach adds an interesting and pertinent dimension, making the issues alive and relevant. Let the festival debate continue and hopefully this volume will help to fuel debate amongst researchers, practitioners and others.

References

Ali-Knight, J. and Robertson, M. (2003) 'Festival City: Influence of festivals on the image and representation of Edinburgh', presentation to Annual IFEA Europe Conference; Journeys of Expression II: Cultural Festivals/Events and Tourism.

Allen, J., O'Toole, W., McDonnell, I. and Harris, R. L. (2005) *Festival and special event management* (3rd Edition). John Wiley and Sons Australia, Ltd.

Cardownie, S. (2001) 'Fresh plans to improve Edinburgh as Festival City', *The Scotsman Newspaper*, June 15th.

City of Edinburgh Council (1999) *Towards the new enlightenment: A cultural policy for the City of Edinburgh, UK.*

——— (2005) *Edinburgh's year round festivals 2004–2005 economic impact study.*

Graham Devlin and Associates (2001) *Festivals and the City: The Edinburgh Festivals Strategy.*

Hall, D. (1992) *Hallmark tourist events — impacts, management and planning.* London: Belhaven Press.

Robertson, M. and Guerrier, Y. (1998) 'Events as entrepreneurial displays: Seville, Barcelona and Madrid', in Tyler, D., Guerrier, Y. and Robertson, M. (eds) (1998) *Managing tourism destinations: Policy, process and practice.* London: John-Wiley & Sons.

ABOUT THE CONTRIBUTORS

G. Emanuele Adamo is junior professor of Tourism Management and Event Marketing at University of Calabria, Italy. His main fields of study and research are tourism and event marketing and service management. Main publications: S. Ferrari and G.E. Adamo, *Autenticità e Risorse locali come attrattive turistiche: il caso della Calabria*, Sinergie 66/2005 ed. Cueim, Verona; S. Ferrari, G.E. Adamo, A.R. Veltri, 'Creative tourism, experiential holidays and multi sensority', competitive paper for the Atlas Annual Conference 2005: "Tourism, Creativity and Development", 2–4 November 2005, Barcelona, Spain.

Jane Ali Knight is a member of the Executive Committee of the Leisure Studies Association (LSA) and of The Tourism Society Scotland. She is currently Programme Leader for the new Festival and Event Management degree at Napier University, Edinburgh. She has presented at major international and national conferences and has published in the areas of wine tourism, tourism, festival and event marketing and management. She is currently conducting research into tourist motivation and in experiences in wine regions; wine festivals and regional transformation and the role and impacts of Festivals to the Edinburgh economy. She has extensive experience in conference organisation in Australia (Marketing/PR Co-ordinator for Regional and Rural Tourism — Strength Through Diversity Conference in Albany, WA, July 30-31st 2001;Member of organising committee for Council for Australian University Tourism and Hospitality Education (CAUTHE) Conference 2002 and World Marketing Congress 2003). She was also conference convenor for the recent 'Running Events in Scotland: International, National and Local

Perspectives' Conference and was conference chair for the July LSA 2005 Events Conference in Edinburgh.

Karolina Buczkowska is a final year PhD student at the University School of Physical Education in Poznan (Poland); PhD dissertation is titled: "History of tourism in Poznan City (1945–1998)". She works at the Faculty of Tourism and Recreation at the mentioned university. Her main interests are cultural and heritage tourism, urban tourism, tourism in scout and guide associations, history of tourism. She has presented at national and international conferences and has published in the area of her interests. Karolina is a licensed tour leader and a member of LSA, the Polish Scientific Association of Tourism & Recreation Animators, and also of the Polish Scouting and Guiding Association.

Dr. **Donna Chambers** holds a PhD in Tourism from Brunel University and is currently a Lecturer in Tourism and Programme Leader for the MSc International Event and Festival Management programme at Napier University in Edinburgh. She is also a Committee Member of the Centre for Festival and Event Management (CFEM) at Napier University. Donna has extensive experience in tourism having worked in the tourism public sector in the Caribbean for 5 years before joining Napier. Her research interests include heritage and cultural representation, tourism public policy, and critical approaches to tourism research. She has published in these areas and presented at several national and international tourism conferences.

Leonida Correia, Ph. D., is Assistant Professor of Macroeconomics and Labour Economics at the University of Trás-os-Montes and Alto Douro (UTAD), Department of Economics, Sociology and Management, Vila Real, Portugal. Her research interests include macroeconomics and cultural economics, with a particular emphasis on performing arts. She has been involved in some investigation studies about cultural events in Portugal. She has presented and published papers on topics related to music festivals.

Sonia Ferrari is associate professor of Tourism Marketing, Event Marketing and Marketing of Places at University of Calabria, Italy. Her main fields of study and research are: service marketing, quality in services, tourism and place marketing. Main publications: S.Ferrari, *"Event marketing": I grandi eventi e gli eventi speciali come strumenti di marketing*, 2002, Cedam, Padova; S Ferrari, *Il miglioramento della qualità nei servizi. Casi e problemi*, CEDAM, Padova, 1998; S. Ferrari and G.E. Adamo, *Autenticità e Risorse locali come attrattive turistiche: il caso della Calabria*, Sinergie 66/2005 ed. Cueim, Verona.

Rebecca Finkel is Lecturer in Events Management at London Metropolitan University and is finishing a PhD in Geography at King's College London. Her main research interest is arts festivals and their social, economic and political impacts on local communities and places. Other research interests include events and tourism, place marketing, culture-led regeneration, creative industries and arts policy. She has presented at LSA, ATLAS, IFEA and Journeys of Expression conferences. Rebecca has researched and written reports to inform the Hong Kong Government about UK cultural industries and policies, and has authored reports for the London Development Agency concerning culture-led regeneration opportunities in South London.

Dr **Philip Long** is assistant director at the Centre for Tourism and Cultural Change at Sheffield Hallam University, UK. His research interests include festivals, cultural events and their tourism dimensions; diaspora communities and tourism; children's perceptions and expectations of holiday experiences; partnerships and collaboration in tourism development and the relationships between royalty and tourism. Phil is a board member of the European chapter of the International Festivals and Events Association Europe and a Council of Management member of the Tourism Management Institute.

Pedro Moreira is a Lecturer in Management and Social Sciences at the Institute For Tourism Studies, Macau SAR, PR China. His recent Publications include: Moreira, P. (2004) 'Stealth risks and catastrophic risks: Risk perception in a tourism destination', in K.A. Smith and C. Schott (eds) *Proceedings of the New Zealand Tourism and Hospitality Conference 2004*, December 08–10, 2004 (Wellington: Victoria University); Moreira, P. (2004, in press) 'Risk taking patterns of decision', Proceedings of the ATLAS Asia-Pacific Conference 2004: *Changing Environments in the Tourism of the Asia Pacific*, November 20-21, 2004, Beppu, Japan.

Ana Paula Rodrigues, MA, is a Marketing Teaching Assistant at the University of Trás-os-Montes and Alto Douro (UTAD), Department of Economics, Sociology and Management, Vila Real, Portugal. Her research interests include general marketing, innovation and cultural organisations marketing, with a particular focus on the non-profit and public sector. She has been involved in some investigation studies about cultural events in Portugal. Now, she is finishing her doctoral thesis in Public Sector Marketing.

Mark Stewart is employed as Tourism Development Manager with Liverpool Culture Company, the delivery vehicle for European Capital of Culture 2008 and for themed years in the build up to, and beyond that landmark in the city's history. This research was completed whilst employed at the City of Edinburgh Council as part of an MBA qualification. Mark has experience of delivering tourism strategy development, new product development, visitor research and event economic impact evaluations — including the 2004/05 Edinburgh Festivals evaluation — from his time working in local authorities in Stirling, Edinburgh and Liverpool and in consultancy.

Xiaoke Sun is a lecturer in Tourism at the University of Wuhan, China. Her research interests include the relationships between tourism and festivals and tourism and globalisation.

GOING FOR GROWTH: DOES EDINBURGH'S FESTIVALS AND EVENTS SECTOR MEET THE NEEDS OF TARGET TOURISM MARKETS?

Mark Stewart*

Liverpool Culture Company, Liverpool City Council, UK

Introduction

Festivals and Events are an important component of Edinburgh's tourism industry, providing a major attraction to visitors throughout the year. Edinburgh is host to 16 annual festivals, annual events such as international sporting events and one-off special events. Each, to some degree or other, is attractive to tourists, bringing visitors to the city, providing product development opportunities and acting as strong components in marketing communications as well as generating economic impact estimated to be in excess of £200 million per year for the Edinburgh economy (City of Edinburgh Council 2004, a).

In terms of public sector investment in the Scottish tourism product, festivals and events currently receive more, and higher-profile, support than other areas of the tourism product where the public sector has previously intervened, such as visitor attractions or tourism information services. This support is evidenced through the total public sector contribution of £850,000 being spent in attracting the MTV Europe Awards 03 to Edinburgh in 2003 and the establishment of EventScotland

---

* _At the time of conducting the research the author was employed by The City of Edinburgh Council and the research formed part of an MBA qualification. The author took up a post with Liverpool Culture Company in June 2005, and the findings represent the author's own observations and not the view of current or previous employers._

to position Scotland as "one of the world's foremost event destinations by 2015" (Scottish Executive, 2003) with a £10 million budget allocation over three years.

Events are recognised at the Scottish level as bringing benefits in attracting visitors to Scotland (Scottish Executive, 2000) while Edinburgh itself is recognised as an international centre for world-class events (City of Edinburgh Council, 2001) where visitation of "festival events" is mentioned as an activity by 12% of visitors in the Edinburgh Visitor Survey 2001/02 (Scottish Enterprise, 2003). This indicates that Edinburgh's reputation as a Festivals and Events destination is manifested by high visitation rates, underlining national efforts to grow Scotland's tourism industry.

For tourism in Edinburgh to develop and prosper, festivals and events have a role to play as part of a product portfolio matched against the needs of identified target markets. Therefore, at the time of carrying out this research in 2004, Edinburgh was apparently well placed to capitalise on the festivals and events product from marketing activity targeted by the then Edinburgh and Lothians Tourist Board (ELTB) at three main target markets — UK short breaks, European city breaks and International Association Conferences.

In that context, the aims of this research are to analyse the role of Festivals and Events in providing products that meet the needs of Edinburgh's target tourism markets. This will be addressed by the following objectives:

- To critically review relevant literature relating to marketing theory, especially marketing strategy and the importance of a product-market fit.
- To critically analyse Edinburgh's tourism marketing objectives.
- To establish the roles played by Festivals and Events in meeting Edinburgh's tourism strategy, marketing and product development objectives.
- To make recommendations on the future development of Festivals and Events to meet the needs of Edinburgh's target markets.

Literature review and primary research

The literature review is intended to provide a critique of relevant theories and concepts within the fields of marketing and the specialism of destination marketing to understand their importance to the marketing of festivals and events which are important components of the tourism product (Buhalis, 2000; Getz, 1997; Hede *et al.*, 2002; King and Jago, 2003; Lee *et al.*, 2004). The review determined the extent of previous research relating to festivals and events and their role in providing a fit to the needs of target markets. Considering the ability to meet the needs of target markets introduces the marketing concepts of positioning, image and the product life cycle that are also relevant to tourism destinations. Beginning with broad definitions of marketing, its theories and concepts, attention is turned to the processes involved in marketing tourist destinations. This allows for a critique of the relationship between marketing theory and destination marketing while also introducing the role played by festivals and events in the promotion of tourist destinations. This approach also enables the identification of any anomalies and gaps among the existing theory.

Drummond and Ensor (2001: p. 9) see marketing as a means to "business success via a process of understanding and meeting customer needs", and the Chartered Institute of Marketing (2004) defines the discipline as a "management process that identifies, anticipates and satisfies customer requirements profitably".

Some common elements are evident — corporate success and meeting consumers' needs — which are also identified by Simkin (2000) who identifies seven common themes in marketing definitions — the ability to satisfy customers; exchange of product or service for payment or donation; to create an edge over competitors; identifying favourable marketing opportunities; generating financial surpluses to enable a viable future for the organisation; utilising resources to maximise a business' market position, and; to increase market share in target markets.

The definitions introduce the concept of an exchange between supplier and consumer, most typically Products which form one of the four Ps originally proposed by McCarthy which remain the cornerstones of marketing theory. In strategic terms, products are managed as part of a portfolio that reflects the organisations' current performance and identifies strengths to build on and weaknesses to be overcome (Drummond and Ensor, 2001).

Godfrey and Clarke (2003) identify the role that the Product/Market Expansion Grid (Ansoff, 1957) can play in achieving a tourist destination's marketing objectives. The matrix is divided into four boxes, each of which suggests a growth opportunity (Kotler, 1997). In tourism, the decision whether to grow via products (e.g. visitor attractions) or markets (e.g. conferences) will play a role in determining whether or not the destination grows.

Baum (1998), supported by Buhalis (2000), proposes that it is possible for destinations to let certain markets decline while new markets are attracted and developed. This suggests that destinations should use portfolio management techniques, and that by effectively targeting markets, destinations are able to develop new markets alongside existing ones. Much discussion has taken place in Edinburgh over the ability of festivals and events to potentially reposition the image of the city to attract younger visitors, such as in hosting the MTV Europe Awards 03 in 2003. This could be seen as a process of market development, rather than new product development at the expense of obsolete products.

The tourism product consists of all facilities and services offered locally (Buhalis, 2000) with festivals and events recognised as being an important element for destinations, bringing benefits in reducing seasonality and managing the product life cycle effectively (Buhalis, 2000; Derrett, 2004; King and Jago, 2003).

In attempting to define events, researchers have identified that they can be categorised by size and by nature. Mega-events are the largest of all, being targeted at international tourism markets (Hall, 1992) and characterised by global media coverage and benefits felt across the whole economy (Bowdin *et al.*, 1999).

At the next level, Hallmark events are so inextricably linked to their destination (ibid; Getz, 1997) that they "become synonymous with the name of the place and gain widespread recognition and awareness" (Bowdin *et al.*, 1999: p. 17).

Getz also identifies Hallmark events as providing significance in terms of image (1997) and also in addressing issues of seasonality by establishing an attractor for visitors outwith the main tourist season (Page and Hall, 2003) and certainly the decision to develop Edinburgh's Hogmanay in mid-winter included decisions relating to improving tourism performance at a traditionally quiet time of year and is now, along with the Edinburgh Festival — a shorthand description for the eight festivals held annually over the July to September period –part of this grouping of Hallmark events.

Major events are those "attracting significant visitor numbers, media coverage and economic benefits" (Bowdin *et al.*, 1999: p.18) with an example being the MTV Europe Awards held in Edinburgh in 2003, estimated to have generated £6.4m in the Edinburgh economy (SQW, 2004). At the time of conceiving EventScotland the Scottish Executive (2002) suggested that Scotland could be host to more major events by providing £10 million funding over three years to attract new and grow eligible existing events.

Getz (1998) proposes that festivals and events are most effective and beneficial to the host community when event organisers collaborate with tourism agencies, supporting the view of Derrett (2004) that destination managers seek to enhance the benefits of events while minimising adverse impacts. Positive benefits can be economic as well as socio-cultural (Hede *et al.*, 2002) although there has been a move to supporting events as products on economic criteria (Brown and James, 2004). This is unsurprising when, as previously discussed, festivals and events are recognised as playing a key role in reducing seasonality, thereby widening the economic benefits of tourism.

To fulfil a wider strategic role, effective marketing will be required to make potential consumers aware of a festival or event. A strategic approach to marketing is required to maximise the benefits of festivals and events.

Strategic marketing has been considered to include market orientation (Guo, 2002) where customer needs and expectations are satisfied (Kotler, 1997) to improve business performance (Guo, 2002; Pulendran *et al.*, 2003). This places the consumer at the heart of business decisions, and the importance of consumers is demonstrated where strategic marketing involves three elements of customers, competitors and internal corporate issues and is the process of ensuring that the marketing strategy is:

- Relative to the current/future business environment
- Sustainable
- Generating optimum benefits to both the organisation and customers
- Correctly implemented. Drummond and Ensor (2001: p.12)

Marketing strategy is linked to the process of strategic management as illustrated by three questions — where are we now, where do we want to be and how do we get there? (Wilson and Gilligan, 1997). This is also true for destinations where destination marketing is seen as a strategic exercise, where Godfrey and Clarke (2000: p.127) confirm this strategic perspective by adding a final, fourth question of "how do we know if we've got there?" to those previously posed.

Segmentation, targeting and positioning are important in marketing strategy as target markets need to be identified to ensure that the portfolio of products is meeting consumer needs. Bowen (1998) identifies positioning as an integrative process involving segmentation and targeting which can be used by organisations to gain competitive advantage, providing a link back to the common elements of marketing definitions. Alford (1998) proposes that positioning is the conclusion of a process where the needs of target markets can be better met in one destination over its competitors and that effective positioning of a destination can make it attractive to different markets at different times through the promotion of different products.

Hede *et al.* (2002) build upon this idea by proposing that the attributes of a destination are used to attract visitors to events, which is counter to Getz's (1998) view that festivals and events stimulate demand. The relevance of Hede *et al.*'s (2002) position is that destinations must understand who is coming to their events and for what reasons (Brown and James 2004), the success of which is reliant on marketers recognising and serving different markets (Arnold 1999, a). Work by Lee *et al.* (2004) provides a comprehensive review of motivating factors for visitors choosing to attend festivals and events while Arnold (1999, a) proposes that festivals serve seven functions: tourism; entertainment; education; social interaction; business; trade and inspiration. To determine whether the festival or event is meeting consumer needs, those functions need to be compared to motivating factors for attendance.

Events can be positioned to demonstrate benefits to attendees, confirming Baloglu and McCleary's (1999) view that marketers need to include motivating factors in their communications. A similar view is held by Leisen (2001) who concludes that destination marketers should use positive images of a destination in directing marketing activity at those segments that have greatest intention to visit.

While the motivating factors of festivals and events need to be identified in marketing communications, festivals and events themselves play a role in the image and market positioning of a city (Robertson and Wardrop, 2004). This positive image can be used to promote the benefits of the destination (Bennett, 1999; Day et al., 2002; Hede et al., 2002) in attracting new markets or growing market share of existing markets. This could be termed market development or penetration were analysis to be carried out using the Product/Market Expansion Grid (Ansoff, 1957).

Jago et al. (2003) suggest that there are strong links between the destination image and the festival and events image with some destinations being more attractive to events organisers than others (Getz, 1998). This suggests that there may be mutual benefits in protecting and promoting the brand values of the event and the destination through effective destination marketing.

Furthermore Derrett (2004) suggests that destinations can be identified by a festivals' brand and that once festivals become part of a marketing message there is synergy between festival and destination. It can be argued that "The Festival" is synonymous with Edinburgh, particularly in the peak summer season and Prentice and Andersen (2003) suggest that Edinburgh has positioned itself worldwide as "The Festival City" whereas Wardrop and Robertson (2004) propose that Edinburgh the festival city is a sub-brand of Edinburgh the destination.

Images can change and are used by marketers in forwarding different images of a destination at different times (Gallarza et al. 2002). In essence this is a demonstration of segmentation, targeting and positioning being used by a destination.

Festivals and events tourism in competitive destinations

By way of critiquing the extent to which Edinburgh successfully integrates festivals and events marketing into its tourism industry, an international comparison is made with Melbourne in Australia, allowing the identification of best practice in both cities. To provide a theoretical underpinning of the promotion of Edinburgh as a festivals and events tourism destination, reference is made to the work of Crouch and Ritchie (1999) and Ritchie and Crouch (2000) in defining the factors that make destinations competitive and sustainable.

Event tourism in Edinburgh can be seen to be driven by a hierarchical approach, where the national agency — EventScotland — is responsible for implementing the Major Events Strategy 2003-2015

(Scottish Executive, 2002). Progress towards this strategy recognises the role that Edinburgh plays in hosting an annual festival programme and in complementing the national strategy Edinburgh has introduced individual strategies for Festivals (Graham Devlin Associates, 2001) and for Events (City of Edinburgh Council, 2001). In promoting the city as a tourist destination, the former ELTB undertook marketing activity that identified the role of festivals and events in generating tourist visits to key target markets. Local actions towards improving the festivals and events product are identified by the public and private sector partnership of the Edinburgh Tourism Action Group (ETAG) and their Action Plan 2004-2007 (ETAP).

Tourism destinations compete with each other and therefore it is necessary to compare Edinburgh's strategic approach towards festivals and events tourism with another destination. In that context it was decided to compare Edinburgh with Melbourne, state capital of Victoria in Australia. Melbourne was chosen as there are perceived similarities between the cities as festivals and events destinations in that:
- Melbourne has a well-established festivals and events tourism sector being a location for Hallmark and Major Events, and
- Both cities stage festivals in performing arts, film, writing, music as well as a Fringe festival for contemporary art forms.

The Tourism Victoria Strategic Plan sets out the strategic context for tourism in the state up to 2006. With particular reference to Melbourne, the city is recognised as a gateway to the state and a primary destination therein (Tourism Victoria, 2002). The means by which the state will be marketed to different markets nationally and internationally forms the bulk of the Strategic Plan, and includes where events will be included in appropriate marketing material for identified market segments, such as visitors from New Zealand, UK and Japan.

The Strategic Plan contains events objectives and strategies, which confirm the economic, positioning and branding benefits from hosting events. Melbourne is described as "Australia's events capital" (Tourism Victoria 2002: p.119) and the Strategic Plan contains strategies to maintain this position against domestic competition from Sydney. Marketing the festivals and events sector will play a role in maintaining this position and the Strategic Plan identifies events as being of particular interest to international visitors as described above. This recognition of the attractiveness of events to international visitors is endorsed by the

Australian Government who in 2004 presented the Tourism Australia Bill. This Bill will, among other things, establish Tourism Events Australia as part of the national tourist organisation to attract major events to the country (Australian Government Attorney General's Department, 2004).

Both Edinburgh and Melbourne can demonstrate that festivals and events form a core component of their tourism industry and that strategic documents and marketing activities are in place to ensure that the sector prospers. Therefore, both cities are working to ensure that one of the key positioning tools available to them is being supported to maintain the city's competitive edge.

A model for the management of competitive destinations developed by Crouch and Ritchie (1999) and revised by Ritchie and Crouch (2000) is reproduced below in Figure 1 (page following). This model identifies festivals and events as a core resource of competitive destinations and therefore if both Edinburgh and Melbourne can claim to have strong festivals and events components, it can be argued that there is a need to ensure that the supporting aspects of the tourism industry are in place to meet the strategic objectives and marketing activity planned for the sector. To allow this consideration to take place a tabular representation in of the Ritchie and Crouch (2000) model is used in Table 1 (following Figure 1) and shown below to compare the extent to which both cities fulfil competitive criteria to support sustained development of an important sector of their tourism industry.

The analysis of both cities against the Crouch and Ritchie (2000) model shows that each is well placed to fulfil the criteria of a competitive city. Comparisons between the two cities are valid as destinations, and their individual businesses, operate in a rapidly transforming business world (Clarke and Clegg, 2000) and therefore should compare their position against competitors particularly where destinations compete against each other for visitors, but also for the right to host festivals and events. Kozak (2002) suggests that destinations can benchmark internationally in order to identify examples of good practice. Both Edinburgh and Melbourne are demonstrated to have well developed festivals and events sectors and therefore there may be lessons for both to learn from each other in the successful marketing and development of the sector. Therefore Edinburgh and Melbourne have the necessary building blocks to further develop festivals and events tourism, meeting the objectives

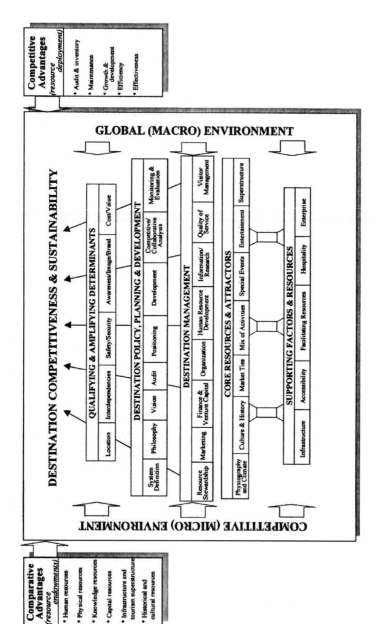

Figure 1: Destination Competitiveness and Sustainability Model (Crouch and Ritchie, 2000)

Table 1:   **Destination Competitiveness and Sustainability for Edinburgh and Melbourne**

Competitiveness Factor		City Evidence	
		Edinburgh	Melbourne
Supporting Factors & Resources	Infrastructure; Accessibility; Facilitating Resources; Hospitality; Enterprise	Factors identified are met by Edinburgh. The city has the basic support factors of a destination in place.	Tourism Victoria Strategic Plan confirms that Melbourne is seeking to grow tourism levels, therefore it can be deduced that these basic building blocks will be established.
Core Resources & Attractors	Physiography & Climate; Culture & History; Market Ties; Mix of Activities; Special Events; Entertainment; Superstructure	Strong relevance in that the city can demonstrate that the factors within the control of the destination are all well-established in Edinburgh. An argument for the Edinburgh Festival to be placed across the Special Events and Entertainment factors can be made in that watching a festival event is a relatively passive experience, but the participatory activities available at the same time, such as Fringe High Street, add to the overall experience.	Melbourne can also demonstrate that the factors within the control of the city are well-established. With specific reference to festivals and events, Melbourne identifies that these form a core component of the tourism product and has appropriate marketing objectives in place, confirming their role as a core resource for the city.
Destination manage-ment	Resource Stewardship; Marketing; Finance & Venture Capital; Organisation; HR Development; Information/ Research; Quality of Service; Visitor Management; Destination Policy, Planning & Development	Edinburgh shows evidence of activity in each of these factors for example in maintaining its UNESCO World Heritage Site status; www.eventful-edinburgh.com as an integrated marketing tool for festivals and events; the establishment of ETAG and its identified festivals and events actions.	Evidence from Melbourne that there is significant on-going investment in the city's tourism industry and that a comprehensive marketing campaign, including the targeting of events to appropriate markets is in place. Targeting of events to appropriate markets requires research to identify the whether in fact the event is appropriate to the market.

Table 1 (cont.)

Competitiveness Factor		City Evidence	
		Edinburgh	Melbourne
Destination Policy, Planning and Development	System Definition; Philosophy; Vision; Audit; Positioning; Development; Competitive/Collaborative Analysis; Monitoring & Evaluation; Qualifying & Amplifying Determinants	Many of these factors for festivals and events are covered by the two strategy documents in that a philosophy and vision for the sector are set out, and go onto support wider destination objectives set out under ETAP. Participates in benchmarking groups of world and European destinations.	Melbourne has the stated aim of being Australia's premier events tourism destination providing the philosophy and vision for the sector in the city. This will be underpinned by the positioning of the city to clearly identified markets for events. Participates in benchmarking group of world cities.
Qualifying and Amplifying Determinants	Location; Interdependencies; Safety/Security; Awareness/Image/Brand; Cost/Value	Evidence that Edinburgh fits well with these criteria in being close to its major markets and in terms of positive perceptions around safety this is evidenced by the safe staging of the Hogmanay street party each year.	As an Australian city Melbourne suffers from being remote from the main generating markets in Asia, North America and Europe. The city is identified as a gateway to Victoria and specific marketing activities are in place to build the city's image in key markets.
Comparative Advantage		The Edinburgh Festival remains a point of comparative advantage being unlike anything else in scale around the world.	Melbourne is able to stage international sporting events such as the Australian Open tennis tournament due to the legacy of facilities from the 1956 Olympics.
Competitive Advantage		Presence of ETAG and the strategies for festivals and events shows that the city is using its resources to build for the long term.	Implementation of Tourism Victoria Strategic Plan shows that Melbourne recognises it has to remain competitive as a destination.
Micro Environment		Factors in the external environment will impact on the performance of a destination. Edinburgh has shown itself to react positively to factors such as the war on terror and Foot and Mouth disease. Evidence that the tourism industry is flexible to respond to external pressures.	Melbourne's distance from generating markets will require it to closely monitor changes in the internal and external environment such as changes in travel habits to ensure that the city has a prosperous tourism industry.
Macro Environment			

of the strategic documents written for the sector and also the marketing objectives that are in place to enhance festivals and events tourism.

Methodology

Completing the research project required the use of secondary and primary research. Secondary research was carried out in order to identify current thinking in the specialism of festivals and events marketing and to identify gaps in information that would require to be filled in order to address the research question. To do so a qualitative approach was adopted whereby semi-structured interviews were completed among an expert group selected using a purposive sampling method, thereby allowing an in-depth study of a small sample (Cooper and Schindler, 2003). Semi-structured interviews were chosen, as interviews are "often considered the best data-collection methods" (Ghauri and Grønhaug, 2002) and are associated with a deductive approach to research where a research strategy is designed to test the hypothesis posed (Saunders *et al.*, 2003).

Before beginning the semi-structured interviews an interview guide was prepared covering topics of strategy; destination image; positioning; targeting; motivation and satisfaction. A process of piloting the guide during an interview was valuable in determining how questions would be interpreted (Sharp *et al.*, 1996) and afforded the chance to modify any questions requiring clarification before undertaking the primary research.

A total of 15 semi-structured interviews were completed among the group, drawn from key stakeholders in Edinburgh's tourism industry, specifically representatives of:

- Individual Festivals covering the calendar year in Edinburgh;
- Edinburgh and Lothians Tourist Board;
- City of Edinburgh Council;
- Scottish Enterprise Edinburgh and Lothian;
- EventScotland;
- The Audience Business, and;
- Private sector tourism operators.

In terms of ensuring that interviews proceeded smoothly, controlling elements were introduced whereby the interviewees' understanding of the question would be clarified if need be. This extended to individual phrases as well as complete questions, and allowed the interviewee to clarify if their understanding was the same as that of the interviewer. Similarly the interviewer was able to clarify his understanding, to assist in coding, the responses received from interviewees.

Research analysis

A qualitative research methodology was selected, meaning that a collection of "non-standardised data requiring classification into categories" (Saunders *et al.* 2003: p.378) was gathered. Analysing qualitative data requires bringing order, structure and meaning to all collated data (Ghauri and Grønhaug, 2002), with there being "many qualitative research ... approaches" (Saunders *et al.* 2003: p.379). Furthermore, Saunders *et al.* (ibid) go on to identify four main activities involved in qualitative analysis as being categorisation; unitising data; recognising relationships and developing categories, and developing and testing hypotheses. This approach allows data to be classified into meaningful categories and clarified into comparable themes, such that key themes and patterns are identified before testing for actual relationships. In presenting the findings it has been decided to illustrate the key themes and patterns emerging by considering responses in percentage terms thereby showing the extent to which interviewees' opinions are shared among the group.

Hypothesis 1: That festivals and events are being used to increase visitor numbers in Edinburgh.

Perhaps unsurprisingly, all interviewees agreed, with common reasons for support of the hypothesis being that Evidence Confirmed Growth (53% of respondents) and to Address Seasonality (27% of respondents). Analysis of responses to examine the reasons given for support of the festivals and events sector reveals that while there is overall support for the hypothesis there is concern over the extent to which this growth is planned strategically, supported by 40% of respondents who felt growth happened indirectly. The overall intention to grow visitor numbers is backed up by the marketing activity at that time by the then ELTB using festivals and events themed short breaks for UK visitors. A conscious attempt at growth by market development perhaps?

Hypothesis 2: That for Edinburgh's Festival and Events sector to meet the needs of target tourist markets, there must be common markets for each sector.

This hypothesis was proven as all interviewees agreed that the target markets for festivals and events — Edinburgh residents, other Scottish residents, UK short breaks, European city breaks and Touring visitors from the Rest of the World — were shared with the tourist industry (excepting Edinburgh residents). The initial analysis was further tested by comparing reasons given by interviewees in stating that festivals and events are important for tourism which showed that Edinburgh's reputation, economic benefits and product and portfolio benefits are key reasons for supporting the sector. It could be argued that if aligned markets between festivals and events and tourism are achieved, then the reasons for support and benefits identified would be demonstrated.

Hypothesis 3: That as well as sharing common markets with the tourism industry, the festivals and events product must meet the needs of visitors.

Interviewees were asked to comment on the extent to which consumers' motivating factors — such as fun and entertainment or cultural exploration — were met by the experience of the products on offer, and there was broad support that motivating factors were met, as shown in Table 2.

To further analyse the hypothesis a cross-tabulation was conducted of identified target markets with perceived satisfaction with motivating factors. An overall positive match emerges, although there is some evidence of a slightly distant relationship being in place between some of the motivating factors and the target markets — for example fun and entertainment does not seem to be a strong motivating factor for European city break visitors.

Table 2:   Extent to which Festival and Events meet Motivating Factors for Attendance

Percentage of Interviewees (n=15)

	Very Close Relationship	Close Relationship	Slightly Distant Relationship
Lots to see and do	46.7%	26.7%	13.3%
Cultural exploration	40.0%	33.3%	6.7%
Edinburgh's reputation	40.0%	53.3%	
Fun and entertainment	20.0%	6.7%	6.7%
Being with others/Socialisation	26.7%	13.3%	

Subsequently, research among attendees at festival events in summer 2004 showed that there was general agreement that the range and quality of experience of the festivals was better than expected, with a mean score of 3.84 out of 5.0. (SQW, 2005), confirming that on the whole the festival experience meets the needs of its markets.

Hypothesis 4: That festivals and events are being used to reposition Edinburgh in other markets.

On testing, this hypothesis is unproven, as there is only a slight majority who feel that Edinburgh is being repositioned in this way. In fact, opinion was split between each of the interviewed groups — festivals and events representatives, festivals and events planners/developers, tourism businesses and customer and audience developers.

Further analysis reveals that those who are unsure, or who didn't agree that Edinburgh was being repositioned feel that there is insufficient collaboration and cite marketing difficulties which would have to be overcome if festivals and events are to be used to reposition Edinburgh. Those who did recognise the ability of festivals and events to reposition the city felt that newly established events had demonstrated that ability.

Hypothesis 5: That festivals and events are being used to differentiate Edinburgh from other destinations.

On testing, this hypothesis was found to be true, with the majority (80%) of interviewees agreeing with the proposition, although interestingly this shows that the split of those who feel that Edinburgh is changing position by using festivals and events is only slightly in favour of the view that festivals and events are used to differentiate the city. In contrast all of those who expressed negative views about repositioning agreed that festivals and events were used in differentiating the destination. This suggests that thinking around and the management of strategic marketing of festivals and events is not clear to stakeholders.

Hypotheses 4 and 5 are important as taken together they represent important strategic marketing activity involved in targeting, segmenting and positioning a destination. This strategic perspective is necessary and is demonstrated as a knowledge gap from the literature review in establishing festivals and events as a strategic marketing tool. In taking both hypotheses together it can be concluded that the hypothesis is partly proven, as there remains significant doubt among the interviewees that a strategic approach is being adopted in festivals and events tourism marketing in Edinburgh.

Summary

The outcomes of the primary research analysis present interesting data in terms of the role that festivals and events can play in the destination image of Edinburgh; areas of improvement in the management of festivals and events tourism and collaboration among businesses and festivals and events. However the research was conducted with the intention of filling gaps in the knowledge that were presented following completion of the literature review and other secondary research. In that context the research is illuminating in that it suggests that festivals and events are being used to increase visitor numbers to Edinburgh, which will be of interest to both tourism businesses, planners and festivals and events themselves, in that opportunities for growth in tourism numbers are possible. Secondly, the research results suggest that there is a close link between the markets for festivals and events and for tourism in general. In addition, the products offered by festivals and events are by and large meeting the motivating factors for consumers of those products. This conclusion is the critical component of the research question as it appears from this analysis that festivals and events do in fact meet the needs of Edinburgh's target tourism markets.

However when attention is turned to the conclusions that can be drawn about the extent to which Edinburgh uses festivals and events as a strategic marketing tool, conclusions are less easy to draw. Opinion is split on whether festivals and events are being used to reposition Edinburgh to different markets, which would have aided the former Edinburgh and Lothians Tourist Board's objective in their Business Plan for 2004/05 to position "Edinburgh as Europe's most Eventful city" (ELTB, 2004, b). However, festivals and events are recognised as a differentiating tool for Edinburgh in comparison with other destinations. Therefore it is concluded that festivals and events are being partly used as a strategic marketing tool, certainly in differentiating Edinburgh from other destinations, but less so in positioning the city to different markets.

Conclusions

The secondary research confirms that marketing plays a role in business performance and strategy. A key issue lies in the establishment of a managed portfolio of products that meet the needs of consumers, and provide financial strength and strategic direction for businesses to follow. As tourism destinations consist of many businesses and operators it can be seen that successful destination marketing relies on important marketing concepts such as segmentation, targeting and positioning, generating a positive image to potential visitors and also recognising the role played by different products in the destination. Festivals and events have a role to play in each of these factors.

Additionally, festivals and events are recognised for bringing benefits to destinations in terms of economic impact and in reducing the effects of seasonality. It is also evident that consumers seek fulfilment in different ways from attending festivals and events, and that different target markets will have their own perceptions of the destination and motivations for visiting festivals and events.

This research confirms that festivals and events are an increasingly important product and positioning tool for destinations. In considering festivals and events as a strategic destination marketing tool with identified appeal to target tourism markets, it is concluded that the literature is less well developed. This provides an opportunity for primary research among festivals, events and tourism stakeholders in Edinburgh to determine the reasoning behind using festivals and events to grow visitor numbers to Edinburgh.

A comparison was completed between the tourism industry in Edinburgh and Melbourne, Australia. From this comparison, it is evident that similar to other destinations, festivals and events are a key component of Edinburgh's tourism product. The provision of different strategies for festivals and events, supported by tourism development strategies and marketing activities provides Edinburgh with an ability to enhance its competitive position in the sector. Similarly in an Australian context Melbourne has established a strategic framework for the development of its tourism industry and places festivals and events as a key component of its product offering. This is underpinned by marketing and positioning activity for the city to maintain its competitive position as Australia's events capital (Tourism Victoria, 2002).

Comparisons between the two cities are valid as destinations compete against each other for visitors, but also for the right to host festivals and events, and in order to maintain their competitive advantage should benchmark themselves against their competitors. Consideration of both cities against a model of competitive destinations suggests that each has the infrastructure and collaborative efforts in place to maintain their advantages in festivals and events. In addressing the objectives of the research, it is evident from Edinburgh's tourism marketing objectives that the roles played by festivals and events in meeting those marketing objectives have been established.

The primary research is illuminating in that it confirms that festivals and events are being used to increase visitor numbers to Edinburgh, further confirming that the second and third objectives of the project have been met. Of interest to tourism businesses, planners and festivals and events themselves, is the prospect that opportunities for growth in tourism numbers exist.

The secondary research results suggest that there is a close link between the target markets for festivals and events and for tourism in general. Given Edinburgh's reputation as home to exemplar hallmark events, this conclusion may be expected. Nonetheless establishing that the products offered by festivals and events are by and large meeting the motivating factors for consumers of those products addresses the critical component of the research question as this analysis has established that festivals and events do in fact meet the needs of Edinburgh's target tourism markets.

However, when attention is turned to the conclusions that can be drawn about the extent to which Edinburgh uses festivals and events as a strategic marketing tool, conclusions are less easy to draw. Opinion amongst interviewees is split on whether festivals and events are being used to reposition Edinburgh to different markets. That said, festivals and events are recognised by interviewees as a differentiating tool for Edinburgh in comparison with other destinations. Therefore it is concluded that festivals and events are partly being used as a strategic marketing tool, certainly in differentiating Edinburgh from other destinations, but less so in positioning the city to different markets.

Recommendations

Building upon the findings of the research and in continuing to address the objectives of the project it is possible to make recommendations for further research and for the practical management of festivals and events tourism.

i. It is recommended that further research be conducted to test the findings of this project. Research among a larger, and wider sample than was possible at this time would be beneficial in testing the statistical significance of the findings, and also whether the findings change by drawing on the experiences of a wider group.

ii. A second element of further research, and one which is fundamental if festivals and events are to meet the needs of target tourism markets, is to conduct research among visitors to Edinburgh. This research can be used to test the conclusions established in this project by completing interviews with different groups of festival and events attendees and non-attendees. It is recommended that research be conducted among:

- tourists attending festivals and events;
- tourists not attending festivals and events, and;
- local residents attending festivals and events.

This will be informative in identifying the extent to which, from the consumers perspective, the festivals and events product meets the needs of target markets. This would be done by explaining relationships uncovered in the research. A control and comparative mechanism would be established by conducting research among local residents as their requirements may differ from those of tourists.

iii. A practical recommendation can also be made, given the uncertainty in the findings regarding the extent to which Edinburgh is positioning and differentiating itself as a destination by using festivals and events. The lack of clarity among stakeholders suggests that attention be given to this factor. However, stakeholders need to firstly confirm to themselves that Edinburgh does indeed wish to use festivals and events in this way. If so, future marketing activity can be designed in such a way that when festivals and events imagery appears in marketing communications, it is clear that it is being used to differentiate the city from other destinations, and where appropriate re-position the city to different markets. In 2004 marketing activity was considered to be pursuing growth via market penetration, whereas re-positioning the city to different, and by extension new markets, could see growth being achieved in the market development sector of the Product/Market Expansion Grid (Ansoff, 1957), and were new products to be developed to meet consumers needs this would be termed product development. Furthermore, an example of where Edinburgh can use festivals and events marketing more strategically is by carrying out benchmarking against its competitor cities in the UK and overseas. To differentiate itself from competitors, and prosper as a destination, Edinburgh should identify its own competitiveness set (Kozak and Rimmington, 1999) in festivals and events. Benchmarking with other destinations, perhaps building on the work included here in comparing Edinburgh with Melbourne, would allow Edinburgh to identify gaps in performance (Kozak, 2002) in how it uses festivals and events as a strategic marketing tool.

References

Alford, P. (1998) 'Positioning the destination product — can regional tourist boards learn from private sector practice?', *Journal of Travel & Tourism Marketing* Vol. 7, No. 2: pp. 53–68.

Ansoff, I. (1957) 'Strategies for diversification'. *Harvard Business Review* September–October, p114.

Arnold, N. (1999) 'Festival tourism development in regional communities — Queensland. Explorations beyond hypothetical dialogue'. in *Proc. Australian Tourism and Hospitality Research Conference*. Adelaide: Council for Australian University Tourism and Hospitality Education.

Australian Government Attorney-General's Department. (2004) 'Tourism Australia Bill 2004', *2004 Explanatory Memoranda — List of Memoranda*. [http://www.scaleplus.law.gov.au/html/ems/0/2004/0/2004040212.htm] (02/07/04).

Baloglu, S. and McCleary, K.W. (1999) 'A model of destination image formation', *Annals of Tourism Research* Vol. 26, No.4: pp. 868–897.

Baum, T. (1998) 'Taking the exit route: Extending the tourism area life cycle model', *Current Issues in Tourism* Vol. 1, No. 2: pp. 167–175.

Bennett, O. (1999) 'Destination marketing into the next century', *Journal of Vacation Marketing* Vol. 6, No. 1: pp. 48–54.

Bowdin, G.A.J. et al. (2001) *Events management*. Oxford: Butterworth-Heinemann.

Bowen, J.T. (1998) 'Market Segmentation in hospitality research: no longer a sequential process', *International Journal of Contemporary Hospitality Management* Vol. 10, No.7: pp. 289–296.

Brown, S and James, J. (2004) 'Event design and management: Ritual sacrifice?', in: I. Yeoman et al (eds) *Festival and Event Management. An International Arts and Culture Perspective*. Oxford: Elsevier Butterworth- Heinemann, pp. 53–64.

Buhalis, Dr. D. (2000) 'Marketing the competitive destination of the future', *Tourism Management* Vol. 21: pp. 97–116.

Chartered Institute of Marketing. (2004) 'What is marketing?', *Marketing Basics*. [http://www.cim.co.uk/cim/dev/html/marWha.cfm] (25/01/2004).

City of Edinburgh Council. (2001) *An events strategy for Edinburgh. Edinburgh — the biggest and the best?* Edinburgh: The City of Edinburgh Council.

City of Edinburgh Council. (2004) 'Edinburgh by Numbers', *Capital Review*, Winter 2004: p. 4.

Clarke, T. and Clegg, S. (2000) *Changing paradigms. The transformation of management knowledge for the 21st Century*. London: HarperCollins.

Cooper, D.R. and Schindler, P.S (2003) *Business research methods. Eighth Edition.* New York: McGraw-Hill Higher Education.

Crouch, G.I. and Ritchie, J.R.B. (1999) 'Tourism, competitiveness and societal prosperity', *Journal of Business Research* Vol. 44: pp. 137–152.

Day, J.; Skidmore, S. and Koller, T (2002) 'Image selection in destination positioning: A new approach', *Journal of Vacation Marketing* Vol. 8, No.2: pp. 177–186.

Derrett, R. (2004) 'Festivals, events and the destination', in I. Yeoman *et al.* (eds) *Festival and event management. An international arts and culture perspective*. Oxford: Elsevier Butterworth.

Drummond, G.and Ensor, J. (2001) *Strategic marketing planning and control. Second Edition.* Oxford: Butterworth-Heinemann.

Edinburgh & Lothians Tourist Board. (2004) *Draft Business Plan 2004/2005.* Edinburgh: Edinburgh & Lothians Tourist Board.

Gallarza, M. G,. Saura, I. G. and Garcìa, H. C. (2001) 'Destination image: Towards a conceptual framework', *Annals of Tourism Research*, Vol. 29, No. 1: pp. 56.

Getz, D. (1997) *Event management and event tourism*. Elmsford: Cognizant Communication Corporation.

Ghauri, P. and Grønhaug, K. (2002) *Research methods in business studies. A practical guide. Second Edition*. Harlow: Pearson Education Limited.

Godfrey, K. and Clarke, J. (2000) *The tourism development handbook: A practical approach to planning and marketing*. London: Cassell.

Graham Devlin Associates. (2001) *Festivals and the City — the Edinburgh Festivals Strategy*. Edinburgh: Graham Devlin Associates.

Guo, C. (2002) 'Market orientation and business performance', *European Journal of Marketing*, Vol. 36, Nos. 9/10: pp. 1154–1163.

Hall, C.M. (1992) *Hallmark tourist events impacts, management and planning*. London: Belhaven Press.

Hede A., Deery, M. and Jago, L.K. (2002) 'A conceptual model of satisfaction with special events: A destination branding context'. in *Proc. Australian Tourism and Hospitality Research Conference*. Fremantle: Council for Australian University Tourism and Hospitality Education.

Jago, L., Chalip, L., Brown, G, Mules, T. and Ali, S. (2003) 'Building events into destination branding', *Event Management* Vol. 8: pp. 3–14.

King, B.E.M. and Jago, L.K. (2003) 'A tale of two cities: Urban tourism development and major events in Australia'. in *Proc. Urban Tourism — Mapping the Future*. Glasgow: Travel and Tourism Research Association — Europe.

Kozak, M. and Rimmington, M. (1999) 'Measuring tourist destination competitiveness: Conceptual considerations and empirical findings', *International Journal of Hospitality Management*. Vol. 18: pp.273–283.

Kozak, M. (2002) 'Destination benchmarking', *Annals of Tourism Research* Vol. 29, No. 2: pp.497–519.

Lee, C., Lee, Y. and Wicks, B.E. (2004) 'Segmentation of festival motivation by nationality and satisfaction', *Tourism Management* Vol. 25, No. 1: pp. 61–70.

Leisen, B. (2001) 'Image segmentation: The case of a tourism destination', *Journal of Services Marketing* Vol. 15, No. 1: pp. 49–66.

Page, S.J. and Hall, C.M. (2003) *Managing urban tourism*. Harlow: Pearson Education Limited.

Prentice, R. and Anderson, V. (2003) 'Festival as creative destination', *Annals of Tourism Research* Vol. 30, No.1: pp. 7–30.

Pulendran, S., Speed, R. and Widing II, R.E. (2003) 'Marketing planning, market orientation and business performance', *European Journal of Marketing* Vol. 37æ: pp. 476–497.

Ritchie, J.R.B. and Crouch, G.I. (2000) 'The competitive destination: A sustainability perspective', *Tourism Management* Vol. 21: pp1–7.

Robertson, M and Wardrop, K.M. (2004) 'Events and the destination dynamic: Edinburgh Festivals'. in: I. Yeoman et al (eds) *Festival and event management. An international arts and culture perspective* Oxford: Elsevier Butterworth-Heinemann, pp.115–129.

Saunders, M., Lewis, P. and Thornhill, A. (2003) *Research methods for business students. Third Edition.* Harlow: Pearson Education Limited.

Scottish Enterprise Edinburgh and Lothian. (2003) *Edinburgh visitor survey 2001/2002.* Edinburgh: Scottish Enterprise Edinburgh and Lothian.

Scottish Executive. (2002) *Scotland's major events strategy 2003–2015 — Competing on an International Stage.* Edinburgh: Scottish Executive.

Scottish Executive. (2000) *A new strategy for Scottish Tourism.* Edinburgh: HMSO

Sharp, J.A., Peters, J. and Howard, K. (1996) *The management of a student research project. Third Edition.* Aldershot: Gower Publishing Limited.

Simkin, L. (2000) 'Marketing is marketing — maybe!', *Marketing Intelligence & Planning* Vol. 18, No.3: pp.154–158.

SQW Ltd. (2004) *MTV Europe Music Awards 2003 Economic Impact Evaluation.* Edinburgh: SQW Ltd.

SQW Ltd. (2005) *Edinburgh Festivals 2004 Economic Impact Evaluation.* Edinburgh: SQW Ltd.

Tourism Victoria. (2002) *Tourism Victoria Strategic Plan 2002–2006.* Australia: Tourism Victoria.

Wardrop, K.M. and Robertson, M. 'Edinburgh's Winter Festival', in: I. Yeoman et al (eds) *Festival and event management. An international arts and culture perspective* Oxford: Elsevier Butterworth-Heinemann, pp. 346–357.

Wilson, R.M.S. and Gilligan, C. (1997) *Strategic marketing management planning, implementation and control. Second Edition.* Oxford: Butterworth-Heinemann.

EVENT MARKETING AND DESTINATION IMAGE: RESIDENTS' PERCEPTIONS *

Sonia Ferrari and G. Emanuele Adamo

Dipartimento di Scienze Aziendali
University of Calabria, Italy

Aim

The present research project aims at surveying how the image of a destination can be influenced and modified by an important event. In particular, the project focuses on Roccella Ionica, a small town in southern Italy, where an important event, namely, the "International Jazz Festival", takes place.

Place image

Place image can be defined as "a sum of beliefs, ideas, and impressions that people have of a place" (Kotler-Haider-Rein, 1993: p. 141). Such images are mental constructs — a simplification of reality — which attempt to piece together essential information about a site by selecting parts from a much wider set of facts about a place and elaborating them (Jaffe and Nebenzahl, 2001). Subsequently, place image is the outcome of subjective perception, evaluation and processing of the wider set of information itself (Leisen, 2001; Kotler, Asplund and Rein-Haider, 1999). From a competitive perspective, place image plays a strategic role in formulating the preferences and buying decisions of potential place consumers, as it affects the public's perception of destination-quality (Valdani and Ancarani, 2000). In particular, place image greatly influences the brand associated with a place and, thus, determines its market value (Jaffe and Nebenzahl, 2001).

* This paper represents, in part, the research project PRIN 2004/05: *Local tourist systems: Place networks and public policies*, carried out at the University of Calabria (coordinator Prof. Ezio Marra). S. Ferrari is the author of the first four sections, respectively G.E. Adamo of the last four.

The image associated with a place is an increasingly important factor in today's market. The construction of a positive place image is, in fact, the key whereby a place can differentiate itself from its competitors, positioning the site as a desirable area-product. If the image result is positive, it, in turn, generates more beneficial outcomes in terms of development of better relations and exchanges on the market, increased consumer loyalty and positive word of mouth. Place image is, therefore, one of the most important resources from the perspective of place marketing strategies (Ostillio, 2000; Selby and Morgan, 1996).

Places need to optimize their positions in order to create a positive image. In so doing, they focus on desired target sectors, attracting the most favourable potential clients. It is, in fact, through targeted marketing that higher client satisfaction can be achieved with a better request-product match. This, in turn, generates positive word of mouth which favours one destination over another. Image has, in fact, a determinant role in the buying process as it becomes a filter through which product quality is perceived and on which expectations are based. In the case of highly intangible goods such as place, together with the technical quality of actual offers and the functional quality of delivering processes, image shapes clients' final perceived quality (Grönroos, 1994; Ferrari, 1998).

In the complex context of area-product, place image is, thus, particularly important since image forms an integral part of the product, playing a central role not only in the buying process (Selby, 2004), but also in the following process of consumption (MacInnis et al., 1987). In the policy of place image building, one of the central aims is, thus, strictly linked to the territorial need of establishing trust, credibility and, more in general, to the culture of an image of reliability and serenity in terms of place efficacy and efficiency (Ostillio, 2000).

Place image is a multi-faceted construct composed of elements which are both subjective and dynamic in time and space (Gallarza, Saura and Garcia, 2002; Pikkemaat, 2004). It is significantly influenced by information. Place image is, in fact, a complex outcome of a conglomerate of numerous cognitive, affective and behavioural components (Nebenzahl and Jaffe, 1991). Place image may often be associated with concrete visual symbols such as local monuments, landmarks and artistic architectural works etc. or with flagship projects, including special events which are renowned and, thus, mirror place identity for both local residents and for outsiders. Such flagship projects come to be associated with a place, representing it and becoming a true place brand (Ostillio, 2000; Caroli, 1999). Of course, the overall image of a place is based on the sum of these inter-acting and inter-dependant material elements as well as on immaterial attributes. These are interwoven in such a way that place image is created not only by specific elements but is also shaped by the overall impressions which are generated by projects hosted by a place (Echtner and Ritchie, 1991).

According to Echtner and Ritchie (1993), the three continua that together create place image are attributes (tangible and intangible), the overall image itself and the components of the image (unique or common to many sites). As for the latter, different sites can be evaluated according to common elements shared between wide areas and usually employed comparatively, and to unique functional or psychological elements which distinguish one or few destinations from others (Echtner and Ritchie, 1991). Thus, a comparison between different places and the subsequent evaluation are usually based on the set of common elements. However, unique elements represent the real factors whereby a brand and an area can differentiate themselves from others. In the shape of famous monuments, mega events or special events, unique elements are specific to a certain place and may eventually come to symbolise it.

Place image can, thus, be considered a true cognitive network of diverse but cognitively linked ideas and information about a place that each individual harbours in his or her own mind, and which can be positive or negative, weak or persistent. Therefore, place image can be shaped by products, events, famous people, specific sites, atmosphere and other components which are not necessarily inter-related or meaningfully congruent. For this reason, overall place image may be a sum of contrastive or incoherent components and may, thus, appear confusing and ineffective.

According to Kotler *et al.* (1993), a place is often linked to a stereo-typical image, or an image which is widely shared but which may actually be "highly distorted and simplistic and carries a favourable or unfavourable attitude towards the place" (p. 141). Stereotypes are basically generalisations and, when a consumer has little information on which to base his or her knowledge of a place, stereotypes become important in the decision-making process (Gold and Ward, 1994). Indeed, once formed, destination stereotypes resist change and provide a simple, although often erroneous, method by which consumers face environmental complexity (Gold and Ward, 1994; Selby, 2004).

Stereotypical images have two main effects on place marketing. First, positively perceived stereotypes are reinforced by promotional information which seeks to emphasise positive place traits in marketing initiatives. Second, place marketing may attempt to reduce or abolish negative stereotypes, directing promotions which emphasise opposite and more favourable, but less known place traits.

The process of destination image formation

Destination image is dynamic and changes in time and space. In fact, the more remote consumers are from a destination, the more distant consumer's destination image results from reality. In this case, consumers must rely on more vague and less concrete information, compared to those consumers who, being closer to the place, can formulate their destination image on more detailed and tangible, if not on more personal, information. This means that destination image becomes a flexible marketing tool. By manipulating elements of destination image which are not only generally desirable but rated as highly important by certain target market sectors, it is, in fact, possible to position or even reposition a place as a desirable target destination for a variety of specific consumer groups.

Different agents which contribute to the building of place image can be classified into the following five categories (Gartner, 1993): overtly-induced agents, relying on information which is explicitly formulated by traditional organisations for advertising purposes, such as information provided by state or private organisations dealing with public-relations etc.[1]; covertly-induced image formation agents which are provided through testimonials of celebrities during promotions or in media articles, reports and documents. Such information is also divided by Gartner (ibid) into two categories: information transmitted through traditional promotional pieces and that provided through apparently neutral media such as newspapers and public events; autonomous image formation agents have also been divided by Gartner (1993) into the two categories of news and popular culture; organic agents basically refer to information spread by word of mouth[2]. Personal experience of the place is, of course, the final and most reliable source of information about a destination.

Policies of place marketing and place image

Place marketing or area marketing can thus be defined as a "group of collective actions designed to attract, to a specific area of the place, new economic and socio-political initiatives in favour of developing existent local enterprises and promoting a positive local image" (Kotler, Haider and Rein, 1993: p. 3).

Until recently, few territories were in competition with one another. However, the spread of new communications and information technologies, the development of service sector and the increased mobility of potential clients have dramatically brought about changes. These factors, together with information accessibility to place goods, services, technology, enterprises and place locations, are strengthening the sense of competition between places present on the increasingly internationalised and globalized consumer-market. European integration has also favoured inter-place competition by eliminating border-controls and customs between different EU (European Union) member states.

Improving place image thus requires the successful implementation of a diverse range of actions such as those aiming at improving public services and increasing infrastructure efficiency, improving the local quality of life, establishing projects which attract investments, tourism, end-consumers, new residents. Even actions which effectively advertise how such initiatives have been implemented, which share their results and indicate whether place image has been improved as an outcome, must be implemented. The shaping of place image, thus, requires the involvement of all stakeholders as all these actions must be undertaken synergistically in a way that the final goal — improved place image — may be auspiciously obtained.

Place positioning is greatly influenced by the vocation of the area and market-demand characteristics. It reveals the political stance of those individuals responsible for building local image. Subsequently, the final image reflects these individual choices which should emphasise and strengthen local characteristics of the area package and, thus, should consider which clientele typology ought to be targeted (Caroli, 1999).

Innovation may also be considered in the process of territorial positioning as it may foster radical changes in the characteristics of place offerings. While risk and uncertainty are naturally higher when innovation is sought, radical changes are, at times, necessary to achieve the strategic place position desired (Caroli, 1999).

Place marketing strategies may, therefore, seek to value existent favourable activities or promote innovation projects. As a tool of place marketing, innovation projects include the organisation of special events and mega events (Caroli, 1999) which have a strong impact on the structural characteristics and image of the area. With increased attention to 'touristization', especially in cities, such big public events, designed to improve the tourist experience, are becoming increasingly important to create positive place image. Therefore, image building often involves investment in experiential marketing (Pine and Gilmore, 1999; Schmitt, 1999), offering sites and initiatives which involve visitors in memorable experiences.

In place marketing, the main communication tools available for building place image can be classified into three categories. The first one includes slogans, themes and positions. Visual symbols form the second type of communication tool used for place image building, whereas the third category is based on events and deeds (Kotler *et al*, 1999: p.169).

The realisation of an important event can thus be critical in establishing a positive place image or in improving and reversing any existent negative stereotypes. For instance, the latter may be the case of a former industrial city which now acquires an image as a tourist destination. A concrete example of such a case can be applied to the city of Brescia. Thanks to the Brescia Exhibition, organised by a local cultural association in response to interest and support provided by local subjects who wish to project Brescia as a tourist destination, the city, formerly associated with a strictly industrial image, is gradually acquiring a suitable image for tourism. Likewise, former high risk cities may organise widely advertised events as a means to project themselves as safe havens for visitors. Such an example is given by Sarajevo where numerous events, starting from the market-fair "Nje ure drejet Ballakani", "a Bridge towards the Balkans" held in 2000 to the 2003 Film Festival, have significantly contributed to relaunching the city as a safe and favourable tourist destination. Widely publicised events can also be employed by seaside swimming resorts which are operational all year-round. Rimini, for instance, due to its high-quality accommodation, is able to host the Festival of Fitness in June, the Sagra Malatestiana in September, alongside numerous other holiday events. Rimini is, consequently, classified as the fourth most preferred destination for Italian holiday-seekers.

Therefore, we can claim that events can shape place image, even permanently. On the basis of the aforementioned place image model proposed by Gartner (1993), events can be considered a source of covertly induced information belonging to the second type. For example, events such as exhibits, conferences, fairs, shows, sports events and the like can have an immediate and significant effect on place image and may more or less directly influence place identity over time. As events generate highly affective and visual impact, they greatly influence the image of the hosting place (Ostillio, 2000). Indeed, public events involve both a direct local audience as well as an indirect audience which learns about the specific area, when following the event via mass-media. It can, thus, be claimed that mass media not only serve the purpose of providing information about the ongoing event, but they are a means to reach potential future place-customers.

In addition to accomplishing an important communicative role by reaching a widespread audience, successfully implemented hallmark and mega-events can also be used by local stakeholders to cultivate interest in the place and build local self-esteem (Valdani and Ancarani, 2000). Another significant effect of very large events can be identified in their capability of enhancing the development of important permanent public structures and infrastructures, improving the overall quality of life and place image even after the event itself is over (Caroli, 1999; Latusi, 2002). Homebush Bay, site of the 2000 Sydney Olympics, for example, was the main structure of the 137 million dollar expenditure and was designed to eliminate nine million tonnes of domestic and industrial waste which was deposited on 160 of the 760 hectares of Olympic venue. On the other hand, the 1,200 buildings of the Olympic Village were completely fuelled with solar energy and following the Games, they currently serve as eco-friendly private residents for approximately 5,000 people.

Finally, it is worth pointing out here that the mere realisation of an event does not always guarantee that the desired place image is attained. In many cases, in fact, if the event is not sustained or followed-up by strategic marketing initiatives or valid investments on behalf of local subjects, no significant medium-long term changes to local place image will stem even from a well-executed event. The Expo '92 held in Seville is a typical example of an event which did not render the planned medium-long term image boost of the host-city. The event, indeed, saw the implementation of large public works and improvements in local infrastructures and services, especially those related to transportation and telecommunications which had attracted investments in Andalusia. However, the image of Seville per se did not benefit from the event as much as it could have, as the efforts towards launching the city-image internationally were definitely weak. Furthermore, structures which were designed for the Expo on the island of Cartuja and which were supposed to be reused as a centre for technological development after the event, are almost totally abandoned today (Tyler, Guerrier and Robertson, 1999).

Some immediate post-event effects can be positive word of mouth (Casarin, 1996) which, if sustained by post-event initiatives could, in time, improve place image and reputation even further. Normally, the positive impact of hallmark and mega events on place image can be obtained when such events are repeated over time. This is particularly true if similar events are offered in small places where there are few other attractions. Obviously, events do not always lead to the generation of a positive place image: if events give rise to negative incidents, such as fights during a sporting event, place image can actually suffer medium and long-term damage.

Event image

The image of an event is an extremely relevant variable as it influences the image of the host-place, the organisational entities, the participants and all the bodies which collaborate in the realisation of the event, as in the case of sponsors. In addition, event image determines the degree and polarity of public and mass-media attention.

According to the model proposed by Gwinner (1997), an event-image is based on three variables: the type of event, the characteristics of the event and the profile of target spectators (see Figure 1). The model refers to the subjective image elicited by an event in specific segments of the market. The first variable — type of event — carries different implications. For simplicity, Gwinner (1997) identifies only five types of events: sporting, artistic, business, musical and festive events. To start with, in the consumers' mind, certain types of events conjure up defined mental images, eliciting corresponding stances which reflect whether,

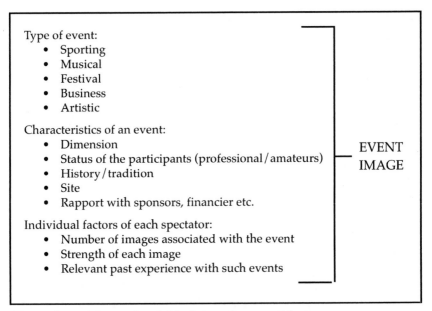

Type of event:
- Sporting
- Musical
- Festival
- Business
- Artistic

Characteristics of an event:
- Dimension
- Status of the participants (professional/amateurs)
- History/tradition
- Site
- Rapport with sponsors, financier etc.

Individual factors of each spectator:
- Number of images associated with the event
- Strength of each image
- Relevant past experience with such events

EVENT IMAGE

**Figure 1   Elements which determine event image
[source: elaborated from Gwinner (1997)]**

over time, an individual has developed a positive or negative opinion of such events based on personal experience or on information gathered by word of mouth or through mass media (Cohen, 1990). Attitude is the background to image development of each category of event in a consumer's mind.

Compared to experiences positioned in the far past, recent experiences have a stronger impact on the event image. Two types of experiences can influence such image-formation, namely, one which is based on direct personal involvement or observations and another which is derived from interaction with other participants, staff or public involved in the event. The first type of experience may or may not be highly subjective, depending on the type of event. For example, the public shares a similar experience at a sporting event while other events, such as an art exhibition, provide individual spectators with different and more personal experiences.

Other elements, influencing event image independently from personal evaluation and governed by the subjective significance that the event means for each consumer, include a set of perceptions generated by the event and formed through mnemonic mental associations (Keller, 1993). For example, the event can generate a perception of youth, advocate a free spirit, define exclusivity, luxury, art, and politics and be associated with other meanings.

A second category of elements which shape event image are the intrinsic characteristics of the event. It is, first of all, necessary to consider the dimension of the event and whether it is held for a localised audience or rather in a national or international context to characterise the intrinsic features of an event. Different variables are at play, ranging from the number of participants and performances, duration, physical space, audience size, media exposure, required costs and investment to the number and typology of subjects involved in the organisation.

Additional other issues influence event image such as whether the event involves professionals or amateurs, the characteristics and image associated with the organisers themselves, the prestige, dimension or nature of the venue, the hosting place and whether the event is coherent with the image of the place, the publicity of the event and if it involves sponsors or other external collaborators. Lastly, traditions, which have been formerly linked to the event, should be taken into account.

Finally, it is also necessary to consider individual elements which define how the event image is subjectively perceived by individual participants or spectators. This is governed by three principal factors: a combination of images that each individual associates with the event, the force by which each image is expressed and the personal experience associated with the specific event.

If an event elicits more than one image in a consumer's mind and if such images elicit conflicting sentiments, the consumer finds it difficult to identify and tag the event, formulating a malleable image which changes continually and is usually based on real-time experience. The complexity generated by multiple images is limited because these diverse and contrasting images associated with an event shape the image-event differently, and, depending on the moment, to a varying intensity with the result that only some associations actually significantly influence the final event image.

Here the notion of past experience only refers to that related to the specific event itself and not the category of such events. If the event is associated to tourism marketing, it should come across as authentic, not created only for visitors but considered as an integral continuum of local community heritage and culture offered to visitors. Examples of such events are those held in Lorient, the capital of Brittany in France where each year, 500,000 visitors take part in the Inter-Celtic Festival, dressing in typical costumes (the Kilt) and watching shows based on the local historically famous Knights of the Round Table and the Ancient Order of Druids. They celebrate and perpetuate the origins and traditions which are associated with the local historical Celtic identity.

If an event is unique, the associated event-marketing image must convey it as a must-see event, emphasising the uniqueness of this event and the importance of participating in person. Such was the case with Notti Bianche which in 2004 became a must-see event in Rome. Modelled after the Nuit Blanche in Paris, it engaged the entire city of Rome in a series of shows presented throughout a single night, involving approximately 1.5 million participants (Getz, 1997).

Eventually, the mental associations, which together formulate the image of a place, are based on several factors, such as organised information sources, publicity, word of mouth, appearance of the place as well as mental associations generated by various entities or subjects related to the single event itself. As previously discussed, in the consumers' mind, each event is associated with a set of behaviours and attributes which are based on a range of factors starting from the subjective personality of the individual consumer and moving to objective information derived from past experiences etc. Together, these perceptive and cognitive elements define the overall image of an event which is then transferred onto the image of the hosting place in the potential consumer's mind. In fact, according to Gwinner's model (1997), when a place hosts an event, the event transfers some of the images which are mentally associated with it onto the place brand. The more favourable, stronger and, above all, unique the images associated with the events are, the more positive the post-event place image will be.

The element of uniqueness is particularly interesting as this can be obtained by combining place with a single unique characteristic of an event or manifestations which have never been organised by competing territories, creating, therefore, the grounds for unique mental associations whereby a place can differentiate itself from competitors. An example of this is found in Edinburgh which has positioned itself as the city of festivals by offering numerous artistic events. The city has always based its offerings on tourist, historical and artistic products related to Scottishness. However, today Edinburgh hosts various cultural events throughout the year, ranging from the Jazz Festival in July to a series of events under the umbrella term of the Edinburgh Festivals in August (ranging from the International Festival, Fringe Festival, The Festival of Books and Film to Military Tattoo Festival) and the Hogmanay Festival held in winter (Prentice and Andersen, 2003).

Several moderating variables can limit the process of event-to-place image transfer and formation. The first is the degree of coherence between the characteristics of the event and the geographical setting and image of the hosting place. When the degree of similarity is only slight, the process of event-to-area image transfer is limited.

Likewise, the frequency, with which an event is offered, influences the success of place marketing. This is due to the fact that, if the event is recurrent and, thus, receives frequent media exposure, event-to-place image transfer is facilitated. However, if the event is repeated only periodically, it is necessary to renew it throughout the years with changes in theme and/or other components so that elements of new attractions are always incorporated. Clearly, the local geographical and historical elements upon which the event is founded ought to remain unchanged over time, maintaining the identity of the event.

Methodological note

The present research project was structured in a quantitative phase and also in a qualitative phase. Figure 2 below illustrates the main effects of an event. The implementation of a similar type of festival has tangible and intangible effects. In the first case, effects are related to the increase of tourist flows, to the opening of new trade facilities and new investments in architectural structures and services. Intangible effects, on the other hand, are related to place awareness, to differentiation and integration of tourist supply and to changes in the tourist destination image. These are the main objectives of the present research study. Moreover, it must be pointed out that these effects do not occur within the same time span, but engage the place in different temporal stages and modalities, as shown in Figure 2.

The aim of the qualitative analysis was to identify the important features and relevant items which define and describe the relationship

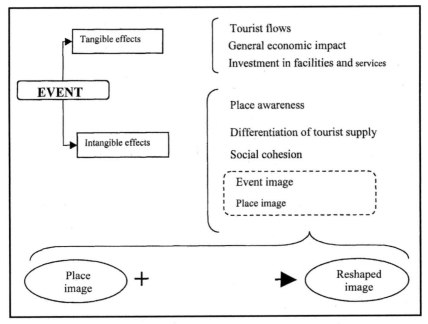

Figure 2.   **Impact model of Roccella Jazz Festival**
[Source: our elaboration]

between the place image and the event, pinpointing the perception of the town-image and of the event. In particular, focus was placed on how the latter can transfer itself on the town-image. Qualitative research was, therefore, carried out to investigate the image of Roccella and the impact of the event on the town from the residents' point of view.

In order to fully grasp an understanding of the residents' perception and evaluation of the issue, the qualitative analysis employed unstructured and flexible methods. Thus, methods, which were easily adaptable to the variety and complexity of the investigated phenomena and to the specificity of the analyzed subjects, were introduced. Futhermore, three focus groups were set up[3], with group interviews on a specific topic, to achieve research aims. The phenomena under investigation regards motivations, opinions, perceptions, attitudes, preferences and behaviours which are produced and affected by social interaction. The focus groups have drawn on the most important items on which the residents build their place-image (Roccella Jonica), their event-image and their perception of the relationship between the two.

The qualitative analysis output of the focus groups was a battery of variables which could describe the image of the destination, the image of the event, the impact on the destination and, especially, on the destination image. These variables have been the object of a questionnaire, designed for the purpose, and administered to a selected sample[4] during the quantitative research phase. As a research tool, the questionnaire also sought to integrate items which had been previously identified during a literature review.

In particular, the questionnaire was structured in two different parts. The first part relates to the image of Roccella as a tourist destination perceived from the residents' viewpoint and uses questions about different targets, resources and quality of tourist supply. On the other hand, the second part is strictly connected with the event and with the way in which it has changed the image of the destination both for its residents and its tourists. By using the procedure of projection[5], we invited residents to identify themselves with tourists and to talk about their perceptions.

The event image

Referring to Gwinner's model, there are three macro-categories of variables which determine the image of an event. Within the first macro-category, i.e., the type of event, the "International Jazz Festival" is a festival, established in 1981, which lasts between four and five days. It takes place every year in the last ten days of August on an annual basis. Within the second macro-category, i.e., the characteristics of the event, the festival represents one of the best-known Calabrian events, even beyond the specific sector of music. The originality and, thus, the uniqueness of the event can be traced in the fusion between the musical ideas proposed and the number of slots allotted to theatre and poetry. The festival profile is centred on music experimentation and creativity. Therefore, the event differs noticeably from Umbria Jazz, the major Italian festival dedicated to this music genre, both in terms of target and programs. Many slots are dedicated to the young and to emergent ideas which have the chance to be performed in workshops and clinics[6]. As for the location, the festival takes place in the town of Roccella. The town's origins date back to the 8th century B.C.,and it was known as the historical settlement of Amphissa in the Magna Grecia period. The town is part of the Riviera dei Gelsomini (Jasmine Riviera), one of the most important regional SLOT[7] (local system of tourist supply) areas which includes 42 mountainous and coastal municipalities. The festival venues are the Municipal Auditorium which seats 700 persons and the Castle Theatre, a modern amenity of approximatively 3000 seats, situated near the Medieval Castle belonging to the Carafa Family[8].

The festival is organised by the Ionica Cultural Association, founded in 1977, which has carried out important international collaborations with institutions such as the Berklee School of Music in Massachusetts. Furthermore, it has established contacts with managers of similar events, such as the Festival Le Mans and the Festival of Yokohama. Directly or indirectly, the Festival has contributed to the origins of other similar events in Calabria, as the Catanzaro Jazz, the Lamezia Jazz and the Jazz Roads of Cerisano. The third macro-category of variables, or the individual factors of the spectator, are henceforth the object of the research analysis.

Analysis of the results

In order to rigorously examine the effect of the event-happening on both the residents' image perception and on their projection of the tourists' perceived image, it is first necessary to analyze the destination image, regardless of the event. It is worth remembering here that the first part of the questionnaire was used as an exploratory inquiry instrument about the place, rather than as a direct inquiry tool about the festival.

Outcomes from the perceived tourist image indicate that, essentially, the town of Roccella has a bathing vocation (64.60%), mainly with family tourist targets (55.26%) and elderly people (21.53%),[9] perceiving the beach and the events as the main tourist resources (see Table 1).

According to the sample, tourists perceive the town as a very welcoming place (average value 5.50) (see Table 2), despite the fact that the quality of tourist information was judged as poor, (average value 2.57) and an acceptable price level was expressed (average value 5.45). Besides, the informants consider that, in addition to the beach and to the events, the choice of the town is strictly related to other main factors given by: the proximity to other famous destinations (4.95), eno-gastronomy (4.87) and the uniqueness of the artistic and archaeological heritage (4.41). While the latter factor appears to have the lowest value among the items considered, this can be easily justified by the proximity of famous archaeological places[10] to other towns and villages (see Table 3). Conversely to the flagship products[11], such archaeological resources are third-level attractions, i.e., they are acquired by the tourist only during the holiday and not previously. Therefore, they do not represent elements that play a role in the buying process. On the contrary, in

Table 1.   Roccella residents' opinions about tourist demand, targets and tourist resources

Items	Sub-items	Values
Tourist Demand	Bathing	64.60%
	Religious	9.56%
	Artistic and cultural	17.31%
	Archaeological	4.91%
	Naturalistic	3.62%
		100%
Tourist Target	Family	55.26%
	Youth	17.22%
	Elderly	21.53%
	Business	0.72%
	School groups	5.26%
	100%	
TouristResources	Sea and beaches	53.90%
	Monuments and Churches	6.90%
	Enogastronomy	5.79%
	Events	33.41%
		100%

[Source:our elaboration]

Table 2.   Residents' opinions on the quality of Roccella's tourist supply

Items	Media	Std. dev.
Residents' Reception	5,50	1,526
Price level	5,45	1,486
Quality of Tourist information	2,57	1,645
Events	5,86	1,379
Gastronomy	5,26	1,763

[Source:our elaboration]

relation to Kotler's notion of stereotypical image, Table 4 summarizes the reasons for which tourists decide not to choose Roccella, according to residents' perception.

The main factors, rated by the sample, are "low accessibility", "scant place notoriety" and "the modest tourist services supplied" (20.2; 21; 7; 20.9 respectively). Furthermore, only 9.3% of the sample indicate the item "real or supposed criminal phenomena". Over the years, this factor has seriously damaged the image of Roccella and other cities in the Locride

Table 3. Perception of the Main factors involved in destination choice. Evaluation scale from 1= low determinant factor to 7= high determinant factor

Items	Media	Std. dev.
Uniqueness of the artistic and cultural heritage	4,41	1,471
Sea and beaches	6,17	1,185
Proximity to other destinations	4,95	1,454
Events	5,93	1,357
Eno-gastronomy	4,87	1,832

[Source:our elaboration]

Table 4. Main deterrent factors in destination choice. Evaluation scale from I = most important to VI= less important, expressed in Percentage values

Items	I	II	III	IV	V	VI	ms	Tot.
Sea pollution	7.8%	7.05%	7.0%	6.6%	15.5%	44.2%	12%	100%
Scant equipment of tourist services	20.9%	15.1%	15.1%	18.2%	12.8%	6.2%	11.6%	100%
Real or supposed criminal phenomena	9.3%	9.3%	11.6%	15.1%	25.6%	17.4%	11.6%	100%
High-price level related to quality offered	8.1%	10.9%	20.9%	21.3%	18.6%	8.5%	11.6%	100%
Difficulty in reaching the destination	21.75	22.5%	17.8%	8.9%	10.1	6.6%	11.6%	100%
Scant destination notoriety	20.2%	22.5%	16.3%	18.2%	5.8	5.4%	11.6%	100%

[Source:our elaboration]

area and has been the main cause of tourists' decision to avoid such destination choice. Although the value recorded in the study does not appear significantly high, it is necessary to bear in mind that the interviewees may have experienced difficulty in providing a response on such a complex phenomenon as mafia. It is indeed, an undeniable fact that the Locride district is often in the news headlines due to the criminal events associated with the presence of numerous powerful mafia groups. These negative stereotypes are resistant to short-term changes and have a negative influence on residents' perception of destination and on tourists' destination choice. Among the elements considered in the gamut of avoiding such destination choice, the lowest value is attributed to "sea pollution" (7.8%), denoting the high quality of the sea waters not only in Roccella but also in the entire Region.

It is probably the presence of such a negative stereotyped image that has induced public administrators to plan an event like the jazz festival, intended as an innovative project, as a break-off element with the local image and tradition (Caroli, 1999). This is also, possibly, due to the fact that the place is not equipped with other resources that could be valued on the market and, thus, could not represent a noticeable differentiation related to the regional offer. In terms of the event and of the individual significance of the event for each visitor, the perceptions related to the event, stimulated by mental associations of a mnemonic type (Keller, 1993), determine the perceived image of the festival.

In relation to the perceived festival image (see Table 5), the interviewed sample has mainly associated the festival with the image of cultural resource (31%). The event has, thus, not only been perceived as a playful, entertaining and socialising moment, but also as a means of enhancing cultural growth which assumes a subsequent broader connotation. The image of amusement and of environmental liveliness follow. On the other hand, relatively low percentages associate the festival with the image of confusion (2.3%) and inefficient services (1.6%), proving the excellent results achieved by management planning and implemention of the event in the chosen place.

Thus, the festival and its image are contributing to the place-image building process, as a covertly induced image-formation agent of a second type (Gartner, 1993). Table 6 summarizes the residents' perception of the place after the event occurred. In other words, data look at the influence of the event on the destination (Ostillo, 2000), by means of

Table 5   **Attributes associated to the event on a scale from I = most important factor to VIII = less important factor, expressed in percentage values**

Items	I	II	III	IV	V	VI	VII	VIII	ms	Tot.
Amusement	9.3%	8.9%	12.8%	14%	12.4%	14.3%	5.0%	7.4%	15.9%	100%
Inefficient services	1.6%	2.3%	3.1%	2.7%	5.4%	8.5%	22.1%	38.8%	15.5%	100%
Residents' liveliness	6.6%	7.4%	12%	14.7%	14.7%	16.7%	11.2%	1.2%	15.5%	100%
Culture	31%	17.8%	10.9%	10.1%	7.4%	3.1%	1.6%	2.7%	15.5%	100%
High road traffic and confusion	2.3%	5.4%	5.4%	7.4%	9.3%	9.7%	25.2%	19.8%	15.5%	100%
Innovation in Tourist supply	3.9%	11.2%	14%	14.3%	16.3%	13.2%	8.5%	3.1%	15.5%	100%
Youth	1.6%	14.3%	13.6%	15.1%	13.6%	13.2%	6.6%	6.6%	15.5%	100%
Pride for the town	27.9%	17.1%	12.8%	7%	5%	5.4%	3.9%	5.4%	15.5%	100%

[Source:our elaboration]

Table 6   **Perception of destination image after the event**

Items	Values
Town of youth	16.06%
Town of music	22.87%
Town with an innovative tourist supply	20.19%
Entertaining and lively town	14.36%
Town not affected by criminal happenings	4.14%
Town with low organizational capacity	9.00%
Town different from the other SLOT cities	10.95%
Town with high inefficiency	2.43%

[Source:our elaboration]

mechanisms of mental association and through the transfer of the festival image to the destination. On one side, the highest values concern the perception of the destination as a town of music (22.87%), a town of youth (16.06%) and as an amusing place (14.36%), all attributes strictly connected to the event typology of a musical festival, whilst on the other, thanks to the festival, the town is perceived as a destination with an innovative tourist supply (20.19%), differently from surrounding destinations (10.95%).

The festival, therefore, represents an element of differentiation for local tourist supply. Furthermore, according to 14% of the sample informants, the festival contributes to the perception of the town as an untouched destination by mafia phenomena. We can, thus, claim that this determines an improvement of the destination image, moving in the opposite direction of the stereotyped image of a dangerous town.

In contrast with other analogous events, the Jazz Festival of Roccella spreads its qualitative and quantitative effects in three main directions besides image: tourism, communication and social.

The graph in Figure 3 shows the economic-tourist impact of the trend of arrivals and overnight stays in the month of August between the years 1993–2003, in the towns of Roccella, Gioiosa and Locri, (the present Festival headquarters). Referring to the event, the Ionica Cultural Association has estimated an average daily presence (number of visitors) of approximately 3.000 units, distributed among the events of the festival

Figure 3.   Italian and foreign overnight stays at Roccella Ionica, Marina di Gioiosa and Locri (in August in the decade 1993-2003).

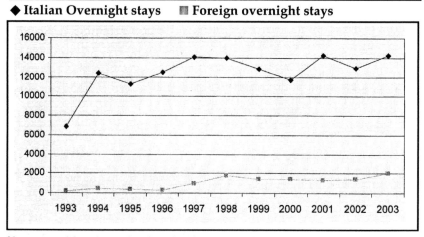

[*Source: our elaboration on data from the Observatory of Tourism in Calabria*]

for the last editions. The graph shows an evident increasing trend of tourist flows in the last decade, particularly in the case of foreigners[12]. Even the analysis of the average stay index for the period considered has a positive value, actually showing an increase in the average stay period, from 7.3 overnight stays in 1993, to 10.8 in 2003. This is deemed as a very high value when compared to regional data and, in particular, to national ones[13].

As shown in Table 7, the present survey shows that the residents have sought in the festival an occasion to extend the tourist stay in the town (average 5.77), beyond the increase of the value of total arrivals (average 5.86), which was equal to 9.467 units in 2004. It must be stated that these kinds of results cannot be definitely attributed only to the festival. We can, however, presume that the event had a great influence on them. It is, in fact, impossible to quantify the importance of the festival in terms of increased flows of arrivals and overnight stays during the month of August, since data on daily arrivals are unavailable. Nevertheless, it is important to point out the influence the festival has on the extension of the average stay. Other tangible effects are also the restoration of the Castle theatre and the development of a series of economic activities connected with the management of the tourist flows and merchandising.

Moreover, the present study has pointed out the perception of a positive economic impact of the festival (average value 5.89), which was

Table 7.   Perception of the Impact of the Jazz Festival. Evaluation on the scale from 1 = scarce impact to 7 = high impact

	Average	std dev.
Positive economic Impact	5,89	1,474
Residents' major socialization	5,13	1,614
Extended tourist stays in the town	5,77	1,421
Increase of tourist arrivals	5,86	1,353
Improvement of tourist image	6,15	1,124
Negative economic impact	1,74	1,437
Deterioration of tourist image	1,72	1,545
Increase in the destination notoriety	5,96	1,437
Investment in tourist and accommodation facilities	4,32	2,125

[Source:our elaboration]

confirmed by the supposed perception of a negative economic impact
with the value equal to 1.74 (see Table 7). With reference to other items,
the lowest value refers to the perception of the investments in tourist and
accommodation facilities (average value 4.32).

Referring to age segments, the association's analysis shows a
significant relationship between the investments in tourist and receptive
facilities and the age segments. The average values of the perceived
impact, referred to this item, for age segments between 14–35 and 35–51
(respectively 4.73 and 4.27) are higher than for older-age segments (3.22
for the 51–65 segment and 3.09 for >65)[14]. These older-age segments
show a major awareness of the low investments in facilities since this
kind of event and its organisation do not demand great architectural
structures (theatres, stadiums etc.) but only simple restorations. On the
contrary, referring to the item "positive economical impact" we note a
positive progress of averages, moving from the younger to the older age
segments (14–35: 5.51, 35–50: 6.28, 51–65: 6.46, >65: 6.45). This derives
from the major awareness of the positive complex economical effects of
the event, acquired with age.

As for the social impact, the festival is perceived as a moment of
cohesion and socialization among residents (5.13). Moreover, the association's analysis demonstrates a significantly clear relationship between
age segments and the item on "higher socialization among the residents", both during and after the event. More than other age segments,
segment 51–65 perceives the event as an occasion for socializing,
although the youngest segments are the ones mostly committed to the
event management as volunteers. These data can be easily interpreted
if we consider that the perception of community socialization is essentially pointed out by people who have major life experiences and major
analytical skills of social phenomena. Moreover, the present survey has
highlighted that 27.9% of the interviewed sample consider the event as
a reason for community pride, following the prominent national and
international importance of the event (see Table 7). This contributes to
reinforcing the sense of local identity, to increasing residents' self-esteem
and therefore, conveys an overall improvement of the image, despite the
bad image associated with criminal phenomena.

The present study, together with the process evaluation,[15] has
demonstrated how knowledge awareness of the festival and how direct
participation in it are extremely high. In particular, 46.72% of the sample

of residents know about the event due to their direct participation in the festival, while those, who have not been directly involved, learn about the event through friends/acquaintances (17.9%), posters (19.09%), TV-radio (8.26%), newspapers-magazines (7.41%) and specialized magazines (1.42%).

Conclusion

Above all, the qualitative impact of the festival leads to image improvement and increased notoriety of the destination. This is substantiated by Table 7, where the highest values can be found for the items concerning "Improvement of tourist image" (average value 6.15), and "Increase of notoriety" (average media 5.96). Consequently, it can be stated that, according to the sample informants, these effects are highly important for the development of the tourist destination.

Figure 4 (page following) outlines the effects on the image-building process after the event has taken place. The festival contributes to reshaping place-image. While Roccella is basically perceived as a seaside resort which covers a predominant family target, the festival enables the tourist destination to be associated with a younger and more lively image which is able to attract new target segments (youth and cultural tourism).

Another important indirect effect of the event is that the festival theme is not related to the current territorial tourist resources. Due to this, the festival increases the notoriety of other local tourist attractions, such as artistic and archaeological heritage and eno-gastronomy. In other words, the festival acts as a window, open on the destination and other tourist resources, since it manages to attract the attention of the mass media.

Such an intangible effect plays a strategic role in the marketing strategies aimed at the differentiation of tourist supply. The strategic role of the event is extremely important not only for the reference SLOT, but also for regional supply, which is known only for one or two famous sites, and is narrowly identified as a seaside resort destination at international level.

Thanks to the festival, the perception of the destination is changing, and above all, it is well promoted. Events, especially those which have an international dimension, can become efficient tools for tourist and place marketing as they aim at valuing a place, and above all, at promoting it. Furthermore, if they target a national or international

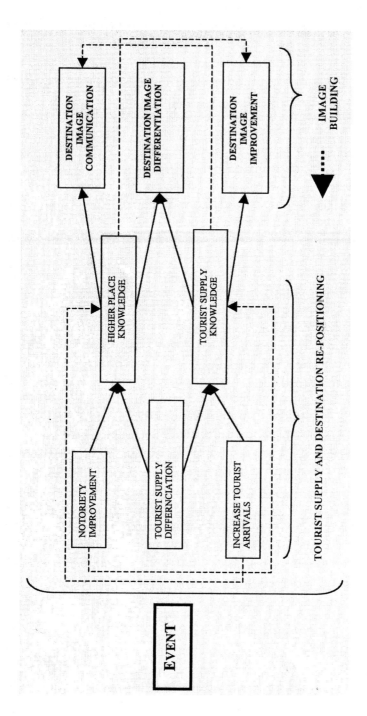

Figure 4   Model of image transfer from the event to the destination

audience, they are surely able to attract mass- media, thus, becoming extremely efficient tools in reshaping or promoting a destination image even if only for a short span of time.

Finally, in the present case study, the role of the event image appears particularly valuable. It positively modifies and adjusts the common stereotyped image which conveys a negative connotation, strongly damaged as it is by the occurrence of criminal phenomena.

Notes

1   They are divided into two classes: *first-level* and *second-level* agents. First-level overtly-induced agents are generated by mass-media while second-level agents are commercially motivated, provided by, for example, tour operators and tour organisations.

2   Organic agents can be *unsolicited* or *solicited*.

3   Group interviews focalized on one strict topic

4   Defining the modality of data record, three fundamental rules had to be followed: the reduction of the lacking answers, the control of the survey prices, and the availability of a short period for data record. The face to face interview respects these types of rules being less expensive and shorter than a postal interview and assures a major correspondence than a CATI interview (Computer Assisted Telephone Interview). The idea of choosing the sample was to guarantee the randomness in contacting the survey units,and spreading the questionnaires in the city centre during three days (two holidays and a working one).

The correspondence was satisfactory: at the end of the survey the sample consisted of 258 units on a total population of 4948 aged between 14 and 70 officially registered (source: *Istituto Nazionale di Statistica*, Istat). Even though the percentage seems to be low (5%), it has to be considered that the permanent population is definitively lower, because of a strong emigration, residence of convenience, and university studies outside the place of residence. The sample units reflect several important features. The cross between sex and age, particular, shows that the sample has approximately the same proportion as the population, except the senior ages which appears slightly disadvantaged. Actually, this is an expected result in which the senior age is more reserved toward written questionnaires and revelation of personal opinions and facts. More than 54% of the interviewed people belongs to young target, because they have major tendency to answer and participate to cultural and explorative activities.

5   Incipit are, therefore, oriented to have a projection mechanism, that is to stimulate answer to the interviewers (about his/her characteristics, habits and perceptions) letting them believe that they are answering for someone else. In that way anxiety deriving from answering for themselves has been reduced, allowing them to answer questions freely.

6   The clinics are jazz schools, introduced for the first time in America in 1982 which, addressed to students around the world allow them to learn, to deepen and to perfect the musical techniques of jazz.

7   The SLOT (local system of tourist supply) is a series of activities and attraction factors which, situated in a defined space (site, locality, area), are able to propose a structured and integrated tourist offer, that represent a system of tourist hospitality, specific and distinctive, that emphasize the resources and the local culture (Rispoli-Tamma, 1995: p. 41).

8   The construction of the Castle, one of largest and most beautiful in Calabria, arise from the XV century A.C. The complex has been built as fortification on a rock, in *Angioino* period and later on used as feudal rock of Centelles (1462–1479) and the *Carafa della Spina* (1579–1806). Its main function, was therefore, defence against the Saracen and Turk incursions, among which the one of the Turkish Pirate *Dragut*, in 1553 is memorable.

9   The business target has a very low value (0,72%) ascribable to the presence of only one 4 star hotel, to perifericity of the city far from the main regional roads and to the poor economy of the district.

10 Neighbouring places have a great artistic and archaeological heritage. In particular *Locri Epizefiri* (680 B.C.) was one of the most famous *polis* of Magna Gracia. Nowadays it is possible to visit *Dioscuri*, *Persefone* and *Stoà a U* temples, while Stilo, the. city where philosopher *Tommaso Campanella* was born, has the "*Cattolica*", the most important liturgic building of the Byzantine period in Calabria (X sec b.C)

11   The flagship products represent the main aim of the journey, while the secondary resources make the journey rich in experience (See Kotler.Fox, 1985; Casarin 1996; Gartner 1996).

12   In 2004 foreign tourism has represented, in Calabria, 13% of the arrivals and 15% of the total presences, compare to a national level of 44%. That indicates a scarce penetration of the regional tourist offer in the foreign markets and a low tendency from the part of the foreign tourist to reach the region, above all for geographic suburban reasons and insufficient notoriety of the region as a tourist destination for the foreign countries. Referring to the province of Reggio Calabria, from which Roccella belongs to, the foreigners' represent the 13% of arrivals and 6% of presences. Nevertheless, the foreigners flow is important because it remains a fundamental component both in flow terms and in spending capacity, and moreover, is a determining factor for stagionality reduction, an endemic danger for the region in which a value equal to 82% of the presences was recorded in the period of July-August 2003. Only in the month of August, while the national data was 21.7% the regional one was 37% with a strong negative impact on the profitability of the tourist companies and on use rate of the receptive structures. (Enit, 2004)

13   The average stay in Italy was 4.17 during 2003, while in Calabria it was 5.7. (Enit, 2004)

14   The comparison of the average values among age segments resulted significant for a level $p<0.05$.

15   Getz (1997) identifies three steps for event evaluation: *ex-ante*, the formative evaluation, for planning and management event activities, process evaluation during the event, for quality delivered evaluation, and *ex post*, *summative* evaluation to determine event impact.

References

Caroli, M. G. (1999) *Il marketing territoriale*. Milano: Franco Angeli.

Casarin, F. (1996) *Il marketing dei prodotti turistici. Specificità e varieti*. Torino: Giappichelli.

Cohen, J. B. (1990) Attitude, affect, and consumer behaviour, in B. S. Moore and A. M. Isen *Affect and social behaviour*. New York, NY: Cambridge University Press, pp.152–206.

Echtner, C.M. and Ritchie, J.R. (1991) 'The meaning and the measurement of destination image', *The Journal of Tourism Studies* Vol. 2, No. 2: pp. 2–12.

Echtner, C. M. and Ritchie, J. R. B. (1993) 'The Measurement of destination Image: An empirical assessment', *Journal of Travel Research*, Vol. 31, No. 4: pp. 3–13.

Enit, (2004) *XIII Rapporto sul Turismo Italiano*. Firenze: Mercury.

Ferrari, S. (1998) *Il miglioramento della qualità nei servizi. Casi e problemi.* Padova: Cedam.

Gallarza, M. G., Saura, I. G., and Garcia, H. C. (2002) 'Destination image. Towards a conceptual framework', *Annals of Tourism Research* Vol.29. No.1: pp.56–78.

Gartner, W. C. (1993) 'Image formation process', *Journal of Travel and Tourism Marketing* Vol. 2, No. 3: pp. 191–215.

Getz D. (1997) *Event management and event tourism*. New York, NY: Cognizant.

Gold, J. R. and Ward, S. V. (1995) *Place promotion. The use of publicity and marketing to sell towns and regions*. New York, NY: John Wiley and sons.

Grönroos, C. (1994) *Marketing e management dei servizi*. Torino: Isedi.

Gwinner, K. (1997) 'A model of image creation and image transfer in event sponsorship', *International Marketing Review* Vol. 14, No. 3: pp. 145–158.

Jaffe, E. D. and Nebenzahl, I. D. (2001) *National image and competitive advantage*. Copenhagen, Denmark: Copenhagen Business School Press,.

Keller, K. L. (1993) 'Conceptualising, measuring, and managing customer-based brand equity', Journal of Marketing Vol. 57: pp. 1–22.

Kotler, P. et al. (1993) *Marketing places. Attracting investment, industry and tourism to cities, states and nations*. New York, NY: The Free Press.

Kotler, P., Asplund, C., Rein, I. and Haider, D. (1999) *Marketing places. Europe.* London: Prentice Hall.

Kotler, P., Fox, F. A. (1985) *Strategic marketing for educational institutions.* Englewood Cliffs, New Jersey: Prentice-Hall.

Kotler, P., Haider, H. D. and Rein, I. (1993) *Marketing places*. New York, NY: The Free Press.

Latusi, S. (2002) *Marketing territoriale per gli investimenti*. Milano: Egea.

Leisen, B. (2001) 'Image segmentation: The case of a tourism destination', *Journal of Services Marketing* Vol. 15, No. 1: pp. 49–66.

MacInnis, D. and Price, L. L. (1987) 'The role of imagery in information processing: a review and extensions', *Journal of Consumer Research* Vol. 13, No. 4: pp. 473–491.

Nebenzhal, I. and Jaffe, E. (1991) 'The effectiveness of sponsored events in promoting a country's image', *International Journal of Advertising* Vol.10, No.3: pp. 223–237.

Ostillio, M.C. (2000) 'La comunicazione territoriale', in E. Valdani and F. Ancarani (eds) *Il marketing territoriale, logiche, strumenti e casi nel contesto italiano e internazionale*. Milano: EGEA, pp.157–177.

Pikkemaat, B. (2004) 'Destination image analysis: A cross-cultural segmentation approach', Conference Proceedings, *Tourism: State of the Art II*, University of Strathclyde, Glasgow, UK, June 27–30

Pikkemaat, B. (2004) 'The measurement of destination image: The case of Austria', *The Poznan University of Economics Review* Vol. 4, No. 1: pp. 87–102.

Pine II, B. J. and Gilmore, J. H. (1999) *The experience economy*. Boston: Harvard Business School Press.

Prentice, R. and Andersen, V. (2003) 'Festival as creative destination', *Annals of Tourism Research* Vol. 30, No. 1: pp. 7–30.

Schmitt, B. H. (1999) *Experiential marketing*. New York, NY: The Free Press.

Selby, M. (2004) *Understanding urban tourism. Image, culture and experience*. London: J.B.Tauris.

Rispoli, M. and Tamma M. (1995) *Risposte strategiche alla complessità: le forme di offerta dei prodotti alberghieri*. Torino: Giappichelli, pag. 41.

Selby, M. and Morgan, N. J. (1996) 'Reconstructing place image. A case of study of its role in destination market research', *Tourism Management* Vol. 17, No. 4: pp. 287–294.

Tyler, D., Guerrier, Y. and Robertson, M. (1999) *Managing tourism in cities*. New York, NY: John Wiley & sons.

Valdani, E. and Jarach, D. (1998) 'Strategie di marketing per il territorio: come vendere un'area geografica', in V. Perrone (ed) *L'occupazione possibile*. Milano: ETASLIBRI, pp. 113–130.

PERFORMING ARTS MARKETING: A CASE STUDY OF A SERIOUS MUSIC FESTIVAL IN PORTUGAL

Ana Paula Rodrigues and Leonida Correia

Centre for Transdiciplinary Development Studies (CETRAD)
Department of Economics, Sociology and Management (DESG)
University of Trás-os-Montes and Alto Douro (UTAD), Portugal

Introduction

In recent decades, the performing arts sector and, more broadly, the arts and culture sector, has been faced with great changes that are shaping the scope of this industry. Factors such as the growing difficulty of obtaining public funds, in attracting resources to maintain objectives, in retaining audiences, the intensification of competition from other forms of entertainment and leisure time occupation and changes in consumption patterns are strongly affecting the ways in which the arts organizations are being managed. In the face of external environment changes, the organizations that work in the cultural / artistic market need to modify their paradigms, references and structures and adopt management strategies and tactics, especially at the marketing level.

Marketing the performing arts and, among them, serious music festivals, is a complex and challenging task. Relative to other economic activities, in this sector the attitude of the consumer (spectator in this case) and his/her interpretative ability are essential. Additionally, the performing arts generally involve aspects related to hobbies, means of personal expression, entertainment, social status and even public policies (Cristóvão *et al.*, 2004).

The main purpose of this paper is to look at some issues related to the marketing activities of the organizations of the performing arts sector, taking as a reference point one of the oldest and most famous serious music festivals of Portugal: the Mateus Palace Music Festival (MPMF)[1],

55

promoted by a non-profit organization — the Mateus Palace Foundation (MPF). More specifically, we identified and analysed the marketing tools used by the organisers of this festival and, simultaneously, we outline some operational marketing strategies for the product market (current and potential clients).

In methodological terms, this study represents a preliminary investigation of the topic, and is exploratory by nature. Thus, the method used to obtain information was based on qualitative research, solidified in the case study. A "case study is an empirical enquiry that investigates a contemporary phenomenon within its real-life context, especially when the boundaries between phenomenon and context are not clearly evident" (Yin, 1984). Examples of boundaries in our case study are that the research is carried out in a single organization and there are a limited number of interviews. Our unit of analysis is an organization (the MPF) operating in the performing arts industry, and we will investigate one of the MPF products — the MPMF.

The source of primary data was obtained through interviews with key staff members of the MPF, namely the MPF president, the artistic director, the public relations manager and the financial manager, and through analysis of the programs listings of Mateus Palace music events between 1995 and 2004. Additionally, we interviewed some cultural/ tourism agents in the region, town council officials, musicians and music critics, to get their perspective about this event (a total of 34 interviews). In this case, the questions were broad and open-ended, concentrating the discussion on experiences and opinions in relation to the festival. Finally, we undertook two small surveys to get some information with respect to the public (spectators in 2003) and non-public (non-spectatores in 2004) of this festival. We obtained 1475 and 874 usable questionnaires, respectively.

After the introduction there is a brief literature review about the application of marketing to the performing arts sector. We then identify and examine the marketing strategies that are used by the MPF for the MPMF, and we suggest some market interventions strategies for each of the marketing-mix elements. Finally, we add some closing remarks.

Performing arts marketing: brief literature review

Until the end of the 60s, it was rare to hear of marketing in the cultural sector (Gainer, 1989). Actually, it was only after the publication of the article "Broadening the concept of marketing" by Kotler and Levy in the Journal of Marketing, in 1969, that the broadening of the marketing field of action to sectors of activity other than the productive ones, was stimulated. This was not passively accepted by the academic world, and only after the 80s, with the publication of the book "Marketing the Arts", by Mowka, Dawson and Prieve, did marketing start to develop in these kinds of organizations (Mejón *et al.*, 2004). The above work "represents one of the first comprehensive attempts to expound marketing ideas in the context of arts organizations" (Kotler, 1980: p. xv).

Many organizations that operate in the arts sector have a negative predisposition towards the marketing concept (Fillis, 2004). In fact, traditionally, the idea of using marketing tools for the arts and cultural organizations was considered to be incompatible with the values and the mission statements of these kinds of organizations. They have been characterized as underdeveloped in this management area, due to their reduced experience in this field (McDonald and Harrison, 2002) and to their lack of knowledge of the market (Scheff and Kotler, 1996). Their interventions are more directed to the area of supply (artistic preroga-tives) than to the area of demand (market). However, despite this reluctance, we can see the sense and the importance of using marketing in this field, and that the assimilation of these principles and techniques is being increasingly manifested (Mejón *et al.*, 2004; Petkus, 2004). In the ambit of the performing arts, strategic marketing has been assuming an ever-growing role, considering the context in which the organizations of the sector develop their activities (Rentschler *et al.*, 2002). Generally, the arts organizations have been getting over the idea of marketing as a threat to artistic integrity (Crealey, 2003).

Despite this progressive acknowledgement, understanding market-ing intervention in this activity area, with its techniques and methodolo-gies coming from the productive market, continues to be a challenging task. The social character (essential to civilization) of cultural and artistic activities, and the contribution to public education and the development of a taste for the artistic and cultural performances that characterize these organizations, make the application of marketing more problematic (Mejón *et al.*, 2004). Therefore, any transference (importation/adaptation) of techniques must be articulated in agreement with the particularities of the sector.

Marketing is one of the crucial elements of arts management, and must be seen by arts organizations as a set of managing systems, in order to effectively materialize their aims and to create a critical mechanism to build lasting relationships between the arts organizations and the public (Kotler, 1980). Marketing creates a better understanding of the nature of the artistic product and the needs and the desires of the customers (both current and potential); it helps to identify a viable customer market and the means to reach it, as well as to define objectives and goals. Therefore, it provides us with measurable steps to evaluate effectiveness (Dawson, 1980).

Similar to other activities, in the performing arts sector there are also issues related to the marketing-mix structure (product, price, distribution and communication policy).

One of the elements of an organization's marketing-mix is related to the *product policy*. The product, in the sense of the number of benefits perceived by the consumers, is usually the point of departure of the marketing activity. The marketing of the arts is different from traditional marketing, in so far as the artistic "product" does not exist to satisfy a necessity of the market. Its existence is independent of the market (Colbert, 2003). In fact, traditionally, the organizations of the sector focus on their supply (their productions, their products, their art). However, and despite the visionary character of art, it is necessary to bear in mind that the essence of the artistic and cultural experience lies in the communication between the artists and their audience (Scheff and Kotler, 1996). In other words, if in fact an artist cannot establish communication with an audience and make his value recognizable and motivational (by reciting, singing, performing, dancing), then each act of performing will be a futility (Scheff and Kotler, 1996). It is, therefore, necessary to balance the two perspectives, trying to benefit both the suppliers and the consumers of the product.

In the arts sector, musical performances are a special kind of product. This artistic/cultural product is at the centre of the creative activity and is, usually, the reason why artistic/cultural organizations exist. Also, the product (service in this case) essentially represents an experience: "an aesthetic entertainment experience made available to the public" (Laczniak, 1980: p. 124). Thus, it corresponds to a set of social, cultural and aesthetical benefits experienced and shared by the artist and the audience (Mowka *et al.*, 1980). In this context we have a product — the artistic performance — that is intangible and variable and whose production is inseparable from its consumption. These characteristics imply the existence of specific problems that these kinds of organizations have to face, namely the predominance of subjective factors in the appreciation and worth of the services that are offered.

As for the *price policy*, many managers of artistic events consider the price to be the least interesting element in the marketing-mix, placing the artistic product (the reason for the organization's existence) at the centre of the creative activity. Nonetheless, pricing is essential for the success of the arts organizations (Lovelock and Hyde, 1980). This dimension brings economic reality to the universe of the arts, for it is the only element of the marketing-mix that generates revenue; all the others generate expense (Kotler, 2000). The price means the value the consumer gives to the event and is willing to pay. It is determined by the level of satisfaction supplied by the artistic event, in comparison to other leisure activities (Allen *et al.*, 2003). In the arts world, the difficulty of determining the ticket price increases since, besides the monetary issues, several kinds of benefits and costs that the artistic product generates can be combined (Lovelock and Hyde, 1980): 1) form benefits/cost: desirable sensorial qualities (look, sound, taste, smell, touch), or unpleasant sensorial qualities; 2) psychic benefits/costs: the ability to stimulate a positive psychological state in the consumer's mind, or negative states of mind generated by the supply; 3) place benefits/costs: suitability and other attributes of the place where the product is offered, or non-attractive and inconvenient aspects of that place; and 4) time benefits/costs: suitability of time and chance to spend the appropriate time in a pleasant way, or aspects of time lost in buying or using the product.

Typically, in the arts sector, and especially in classical music, due to its social and economic profile, the target market segment is assumed to have little interest in the price (Frey, 2003). Obviously, if the objective is to get to new audiences, for instance adolescents, attention should be paid to this element, seeing that in this group there is already a strong awareness of cost. As for the value that should be charged for the artistic events, reality shows that, although producers are facing increasing costs, from the perspective of those who buy the ticket, there are factors for prices to be reduced (Lovelock and Hyde, 1980), especially because they are public goods, that generate positive externalities in the production and consumption, whose counterpart is the public financing of the cultural performing activities, capable of covering the market flaw, and furthermore, increasing the supply/consumption of these goods. The lack of such a public subsidy creates an undersupply of the good.

The *distribution policy* comprises the set of systems, methods and techniques that allow and facilitate the product offer to the target public. In the context of artistic/cultural services marketing, there is simultaneity between the production and the consumption of the product, which leads to the analysis of specific variables, such as the supply place, the interior and exterior look of that place and the conditions of ticket acquisition. The success of music festivals is intimately related to the location where they take place. For example, people from low formal education groups and with little cultural tradition, normally, feel intimidated, insecure and unwelcome in "culture temples" such as opera houses and concert rooms, contrary to how they feel in "public spaces", such as churches or gardens, which are accessible and attractive to the majority of the population (Frey, 2003).

In the context of the performing arts sector, the *communication policy* plays an essential role in attracting and maintaining the audiences necessary for the success and survival of the organizations that work in this market (Strang and Gutman, 1980).The artistic/cultural organizations, in the development of their activities, directly or indirectly interact with a diverse public, and they should be concerned with the signs they are transmitting to them. In this regard, it is important to analyse some essential stages of the communication process:

1) who communicates? (who are the sources?);
2) to whom? (who are the targets?);
3) what? (which messages to transmit?);
4) how? (through which channels?), that is to say, the set of available forms of communication (advertising, public relations, sales promotions, direct marketing, etc);
5) where and when? (media plan); and
6) with what results? (were the objectives achieved?).

It is worth noting that the communication objectives inherent in this sector will have a strong education component, besides the usual objectives of information and persuasion, respectively for the segments of non-participants, enthusiasts and interested people.

MPMF marketing strategy

The MPMF is deeply related to the history, property and management of the Mateus Palace (situated in Vila Real), which is considered to be one of the most representative Baroque monuments in Northern Portugal, and one of the most characteristic in Europe, having been classified as a national monument in 1911. The Mateus Palace Foundation is a non-profit institution that was instituted in 1970, with cultural, artistic, educative and scientific purposes and which, since 1985, has organised the Mateus Palace Music Festival.

In relation to the MPMF, the MPF intends to (1) contribute to the external promotion of the region; (2) give the local population the possibility of appreciating some of the most acclaimed interpreters of serious music of the present time, in their home towns, thus helping the cultural development of this region; and (3) give value to the local cultural spaces and heritage through cultural animation and documentation, thus contributing to the development of tourism in the North of Portugal. The main targets are the local populations, national and foreign visitors, students and professionals in the music field.

The MPMF takes place in the summer time, and lasts longer (between two to three months) than any other current serious music festival in Portugal. Also, it covers a larger area, given that the concerts take place in several localities in Northern Portugal: out of 412 concerts held between 1995 and 2004, 42% took place in Mateus Palace (the MPF site) and 58% in other locations in the region. Globally, during the analysis period, 39 locations were covered, 36 of them in Northern Portugal.

As we mentioned, the adoption of marketing by the performing arts organizations has been slow, despite their acknowledgement of the importance of marketing as a management tool (Rentschler, 2002). The MPF has not been unaware of this tendency. Similar to other artistic/cultural organizations, the MPF has been facing several problems, from the reduction of public financial support to the decrease of audiences, and the growing competition of other ways of spending available leisure time. In order to guarantee its continuity, the MPF realises that it is necessary to change several aspects, including marketing and the way it develops the audiences. Therefore, the MPF objectives, considering one of its main groups of interest — the users' market (current and potential clients) — are to increase total participation in the event, to increase the loyalty rate in participation, and to reinforce the brand image of the MPMF.

In this section, we first identify the set of strategies, at the marketing-mix level, adopted by the MPF for the MPMF. We simultaneously outline some market intervention alternatives for this product, for each of the items studied. The proposed actions are mainly incremental changes, compatible with the economic and financial limitations of the MPF.

MPMF Market

Market knowledge plays an essential role in marketing activity and is a point of departure for the decision-making and the development of any marketing strategy and action program. Up until the researches carried out by Cristovão *et al.* (2003, 2004), the MPF had never developed systematic studies into who constitutes its market (current and potential clients), and it had never used essential marketing components such as market research, segmentation of that market and analysis of competition.

The information obtained through the analysis of the programs listings of Mateus Palace music events, between 1995 and 2004, allow us to conclude that the number of spectators has been significant, but decreasing. For instance, in 1999 the number of spectators per concert in events that were held outside the MPF site (Mateus Palace) was 218, and in 2004, it was 120, with an average occupancy of the rooms of 90% and 69%, respectively. For the concerts that took place at the Mateus Palace, in 2003 and 2004, the number of spectators was 1400 and 1361 respectively, which when compared with the number of concerts (13 and 19) gave an average number of 108 and 72 spectators per concert.

Nowadays it is fundamental that the arts organizations assume a dynamic adaptation attitude to the markets placing themselves closer and closer to their target public. Therefore, it is necessary to know them as well as possible, in order to identify the areas where one should "invest", that is to say, direct communication and the supply of products and services more effectively.

Through two studies[2] carried out at different times, and through the survey method, we have obtained information on the public and the non-public of this festival, whose main conclusions are described below.

• MPMF public (2003 season)

In the first study (Cristóvão *et al.*, 2003), we made a characterization of the festival's spectators (2003 season), from the survey of the individuals making their way to the place of the concert, and we obtained 1475 usable questionnaires.

In terms of socio-economical characterization, the spectator profile revealed that the majority of the respondents belong to the female sex, to a group aged between 20 to 30, were college graduates, married, of

Portuguese nationality and lived in the districts of Porto or Vila Real. We noticed that the majority had an average income per mouth between 1000¤ to 2000¤ and, in terms of main occupation/pr ofession, the senior staff and the students stand out.

Relative to aspects directly related to the festival, the following general conclusions are: 1) the greater part of the spectators were participating in this event for the first time (62.7%) while the frequent concert-goers were only 12% of the total questioned; 2) the respondents learned about the festival, essentially, through their family and/or friends, through posters/leaflets and through the press (almost 90% of the total); 3) the majority of the individuals (65%) positively evaluated the effectiveness of the communication means used, however, respondents not knowing the whole festival program prevailed (63%); 4) the greater part of the individuals (73%) intended to participate in the next festival season. This information allows us to recognize a positive appreciation of the event by those attending, which is an important sign of public loyalty, considering that most were participating for the first time; 5) in terms of price, generally the literature mentions that the audiences of serious performances are not very sensitive to this factor. In the case being analysed, more than 58% of those attending (only in the concerts taking place at the Mateus Palace) classified the ticket price as reasonable while for 28% and 14% the price was high and low, respectively; and 6) the spectators' main motivations for participating were related to the "place of the concerts", to "the whole program" of the shows, or to a "particular soloist, orchestra or group". The "services offered" by the organization appeared as one of the least mentioned alternatives.

• MPMF non-public (2004 season)

In the second study (Cristóvão'*et al.*, 2004), which was carried out during the 2004 season, we sought to discover and analyse the behaviour of the "non-spectators[3]", that is to say, those who, at the moment when the inquiry was being held, were engaged a certain leisure activity (socializing in an open-air cafe; watching a film at the cinema; watching a play, a musical show or a dance performance in the theatre), and were not attending the concerts of the festival, taking place at the same time. We have obtained 874 usable questionnaires.

In terms of socio-economic characterization of the respondents, the following profile was revealed: the majority belonged to the female sex, to the young-adult age group (21 to 30 years of age), was single and studied or worked as a specialist of intellectual and scientific professions or as a technician and professional of intermediate level, was a college graduate, resided in the Vila Real area and enjoyed a low income per month (below 1000 and between 1001 and 2000¤).

From the relationship between the respondents and the MPMF, we noticed that: 1) nearly 64% knew or had heard of the MPMF, although the greater part of the respondents (nearly 76%) had never attended a concert of this festival; 2) almost all the respondents (93%) did not know what was the event of the festival taking place at the time of the inquiry; 3) the majority of the respondents (86%) did not intend to participate in events of the MPMF. The main reasons for not participating were related to "not knowing the program", the "high price", the "not of the area", and "not liking the kind of music"; and 4) the remaining 14% of the respondents that intended to attend performances of the festival, chose classical music concerts, followed by jazz, "fado" and, lastly, baroque/ancient music.

The information obtained from the two investigations allows us to define two segments that require different treatment in terms of marketing-mix variables. On the one hand, we have the segment of those who have already participated, composed of those that have been enthusiastic with regard to the festival, and show great interest in the event (subsegment of the "frequent clients"); and those that have an inferior level of involvement, appearing to be less interested in the event (sub segment of the "occasional clients"). In these two sub segments, adults and seniors citizens[4] (31 –40; 41 — 50; 51 and up), belonging to the upper classes, middle/upper classes and middle classes prevail.

On the other hand, there is the segment of the "non-participants", composed of individuals that did not participate at the time when the inquiry was taking place. We can also subdivide this segment into the group of those who did not know about the festival and the group of those who knew about it but did not use the product at that moment, in particular, the subsegment of children, adolescents and young adults[5].

In market analysis, it is important to look at the essential conditions of the business that come from the external environment and are indispensable to any marketing strategic planning. Thus, considering the opportunities this festival is facing, we point out the following aspects that the MPF should take into account:

- The location: it takes place in the Douro area, recently classified as a World Heritage Site by UNESCO which, consequently, should increase the tourist interest;
- The possibility of association with other famous regional products, so as to generate more cohesion and competitivity in the territory, higher receptivity in the community and the strengthening of interconnections with other national, regional and local entities;
- The improvement of access to the region by air and overland, and the important cultural facilities that have recently opened (Municipal Theatre, Regional Conservatory of Music and the new Municipal Library);
- The opening of a new course in UTAD of "Theatre and Performing Arts" which, together with the new cultural facilities creates a favourable environment for the creation of a culture cluster and conditions suitable to the affirmation of this region as a pole of music creation and diffusion; and
- A more favourable legislation in terms of patronage of the arts, mainly in terms of more alluring tax incentives for sponsors.

On the other hand, the threats to this product are:
- The Municipal Theatre of Vila Real which, although being able to work as a complementary structure and even be included in the festival, on the other hand, can represent a threat to this event and mainly to the attraction of new audiences, once it becomes a competitor in cultural events, not only in the music area; it appears as an alternative way of spending spare time for the locals;
- The opening of new space for leisure activities that may render difficult the acquisition of new audiences for the festival, particularly from the segment of young spectators that tend to be less identified with the MPMF;
- The constant appearance of initiatives at a regional/north and national level in the field of music festivals;
- The low purchasing power of the region's inhabitants, which is lower than the national average, associated with a low sensitivity to the "cultural product" making them non-consumers of serious musical events; and
- The restricted quantity of the accommodation and food services of the area, which limits the number of visitors.

The Marketing-mix

In this section we are going to approach traditional variables that make part of the marketing-mix (product, price, distribution and communication policy).

Product Policy

In this regard, besides the core service, it is important to analyse the primary/essential peripheral services and the augmented peripheral services (see Figure 1).

The MPMF central service is related to its mission/vocation, and concerns the artistic performance itself that is presented in each concert of the annual program (or series of concerts included in a season).

As to the kind of music, the festival has been offering some diversity of concerts, from ancient to contemporary and from erudite to popular music. However, classical, baroque music and jazz have been assuming a special place. The introduction of other musical types such as "fado", Brazilian popular music or pop music, is one of the innovative aspects

Figure 1   The three levels of the product: application to the MPMF

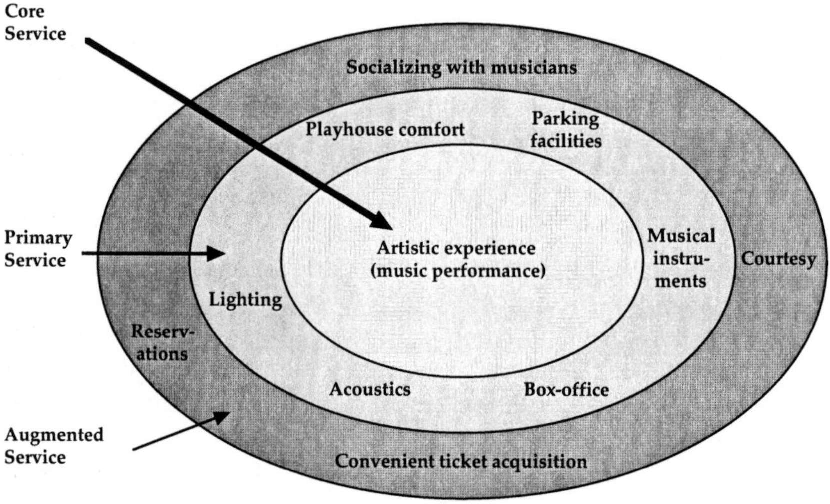

(Source: Adapted from Kotler and Armstrong, 1993)

we can find in the festival evolution, transforming it into a plural event where there is room for different repertoires and diverse audiences.

The program definition for each festival season has been the responsibility of an artistic director, together with the president of the foundation. The MPF maintains a close friendship and collaboration with a group of famous international musicians, who have been participating in this festival on a regular basis (e.g.: Jacques Ogg, Max van Egmond, Jacob Lindberg, Gustav Leonhardt, Cristian Mendoze, Lorraine Nubal, Dalton Baldwin, Teresa Berganza). This close relationship is a reason for the reduction of expenses with the artists who, in this festival, usually charge smaller fees, but has been contributing to some limitations in the program as time goes by.

Besides the core product, the primary services comprise the set of normal expectations related to the product consumption (e.g.: the environment, room comfort, illumination, good acoustic quality, warm reception at the box-office, parking facilities). We pointed out that the MPF should consciously manage, as a part of the product, these peripheral elements of the event.

The augmented services complete the value given to the product. Considering that the MPMF is, according to the concept of the product's life cycle, in its mature phase, these additional services play an essential role because, usually, there is a displacement of the competition from the product itself to an emphasis on the consumer service and secondary benefits. Therefore, it is fundamental to keep the clients (loyalty policies), discover new markets (by adapting the product), and to extend the product's life period (for example, by developing a special effort to attract adolescents).

In terms of positioning, the MPMF is perceived by the festival promoter as having some distinctive characteristics (Cristóvão *et al.*, 2003). According to MPF, tradition, erudition and quality are the main vectors of the MPMF position in the market (Figure 2).

The essence of this product is related to the unquestionable quality of the performers and with their level of eclecticism. This idea is supported by the results obtained from the interviews with various external agents (musicians, critics, political representatives, cultural and tourist agents). In their opinion, the MPF is a good organizer of the festival, and produces, with a very light and flexible organizational structure, a product of undisputed quality with relatively low costs of production. The MPMF is unanimously recognized, by several respondents, as one

Figure 2   MPMF positioning diagram

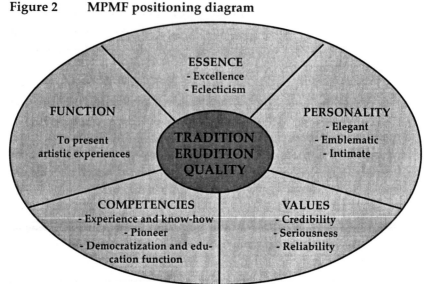

(Source: Adapted from Brochand *et al.*, 1999)

of the best serious music festivals in Portugal. In terms of distinctive factors, in accordance with the heard opinions, the differentiation of the product seems to be for the following reasons: (1) the quality of the musicians; (2) the physical and human amenity of the main place site of the event and its emblem — the Palace of Mateus; (3) the link to other activities organized by the MPF (e.g. International Courses of Music); and (4) the area covered by, with diverse and unorthodox public integration.

With regard to the "personality" of the event, we may say it is one that offers singular, embracing and intimate experiences, representing an emblematic event for the region. Values such as credibility and seriousness are also characteristics of this product.

As for the product's competence, the MPMF counts on wide experience and know-how to promote it in the serious music arena. On the other hand, besides being an artistic/cultural product of unquestionable quality in the national (and international) music environment, it was also a pioneer, in Portugal, in the area of baroque music.

From the agent's perspective this initiative is admittedly a value-added for the region, being its most important cultural event. Collected opinions support the idea that the festival reinforces regional identity and cohesion, contributes to the promotion of the region, its cultural heritage, and to the formation of the music preferences of the residents. This event is clearly a success in terms of cultural democratization and a unique opportunity for the dissemination of serious music in a rural region.

Finally, it is necessary to define strategies to enlarge the product and to respond to environment changes. Thus, sharing the opinion that balance should be kept between the interests of the organization and the interests of the sector and the market, we mention some development possibilities for the MPMF:

- *To introduce a specific program for children* (together with their parents) We know that, besides the values that are passed on by family and schools, the exposure of children to the arts and its practice as amateurs, represent factors that influence adult cultural preferences. Moreover, it is believed that these preferences are established before the age of 20 (Colbert, 2003). Therefore, it is important to draw children's attention to the arts. The introduction of a program (two to three concerts per year) especially directed to children will meet this need. Thus, the role of educating and creating the taste for music of this kind would be emphasised;
- *To get to the segment of the young or young adults by introducing music concerts that appeal to them.* By keeping the strict criteria that have been associated with the selection of musicians, and not turning away from the guidelines of the festival, it is possible to diversify the offer to this segment, to introduce innovations into the program, and extend the contacts network and demystify critics' opinion about the possibility of some program repetition. The market tendencies should be identified and followed if possible, otherwise there is a risk of a continuing slow decline in audiences;
- *To organize thematic concerts.* Whenever possible, concerts according to a musical kind, an artist or a season should be promoted; and
- *To organize outdoor concerts.* That way, the problem of limited room space would be solved and audience numbers would grow.

Price Policy

For the organisers of the festival, the attraction and creation of funds is an essential activity. In economic and financial terms, the main supporters of the MPMF are the European Regional Development Fund, public and private entities, and the ticket revenues of the concerts held at the Mateus Palace (only events in the Mateus Palace are charged for;

in the remaining localities where the events take place, admission is free). It is worth mentioning the high dependence on public funds considering that the private funds represent just 17% of the total subsidies received by the MPF. As for the ticket revenues, during the period that was analysed, we verified an amount of 3% of the total expenses of the festival. The expenses related to promoting and divulging the product represent nearly 16% of the total direct costs.

The price policy corresponds to a critical element in the whole organization's marketing program. With regard to the ticket price, the MPF imposes the following practices: 1) the use of a discount price policy, charging lower prices to the young and senior citizens; and 2) the application of different prices according to the expenses involved in the organization of each specific concert. The tickets for the MPMF concerts are sold exclusivity on the premises, and the payment has to be made in cash.

In this context, in order to increase ticket sales, we suggest the following changes: 1) in the situations where the concert rooms have "good" and "bad" places, there should be different prices according to seat location; 2) to charge lower prices certain days of the week and higher prices during the weekend; and 3) to charge different prices for tourists.

Distribution policy

Each product, according to its characteristics, requires different forms of distribution. As this product is mainly an intangible good (service), the channel of distribution is usually transformed at the place of supply, where the production, the point of sale, and the use/consumption are simultaneously united. Given this simultaneity, it is essential to analyse all the problems related to the spatial location of the events.

In this case there are two situations: the concerts that take place at the Mateus Palace, and the concerts that take place in other localities. The first ones benefit from a symbolic, historical and magical context that adds value to the product. In Mateus Palace the concerts are given in relatively small rooms, which turns them into intimate performances, directed at selected audiences. In the events that take place elsewhere, the MPF does not always manage to control this factor as they would wish. These concerts happen in very different spaces, from the architectural point of view (manor houses, churches, auditoriums), from a geographical point of view (dispersion in terms of territory), and in a context where the space alternatives are restricted (as well as related aspects, for example, the availability of musical instruments). This might imply unfavourable conditions for the public in general and even for the musicians. Therefore, it is necessary to reconsider the current model of the festival, relative to the geographical dispersion. Our suggestion is that the concerts should be concentrated in their home territory.

Apart from the place of product supply, it is important to analyse all the issues related to the environment, the acoustic conditions, illumination, room capacity, comfort and the means of ticket acquisition (only at the entrance door or in other locations) and respective payment, which are also associated to the product policy. The tickets for the Mateus Palace concerts are sold exclusively on the premises, and payment has to be made in cash. Therefore, with the purpose of facilitating and making more convenient the consumption of the product MPMF, we suggest the following actions:

- Partially delegate some of the tasks related to information giving, booking and ticket purchase to specialist agencies (e.g. travel and tourist agencies), and to city shops, accessible to the majority of people from the target area (e.g. main streets, shopping centre, stores, theatre, among others);
- In order to offer more convenience in payment, a system of purchase and booking of tickets by telephone or through the internet should be implemented for clients paying with credit cards; and to allow payment by cheque or electronic money at the box-office; and
- The creation and maintenance, in a systematic and consistent way, of a web page. The internet, besides being an important means of communication, also works as a channel of distribution. One of the main advantages related to this tool lies in the possibility of building a relationship with the client, as a consequence of the interactivity. Thus, we would be investing in a direct channel of distribution to potential clients.

Communication policy

In the context of the communication policy, it is important to analyse the communication objectives, the targets, the kinds of communication and the means available to reach clients. The communication objectives of the MPF can be grouped into three main goals: 1) to inform (e.g. on the events, dates, place, ticket price, how to get the tickets); 2) to persuade (incentives to encourage participation), and 3) lead to action (participation). The education element assumes a special importance given that, for the majority of people, the appreciation of serious music is learned or acquired over time (Strang and Gutman, 1980). This implies that audience expansion requires the development of a level of understanding that motivates participation in similar events.

Besides the marketing targets (current and potential clients), the communication targets broadly include all the individuals that may influence the MPF activities; in other words, the sponsors/donors, the State, the local community, the media, the reference groups, among others. In this case, the main way through which participants took notice of the festival was through their family and/or friends, which also reflects the importance of the reference groups (primary and secondary), and of word of mouth in influencing clients' behaviour towards their participation (or not) in events of this kind.

As for the kind of communication, the product/brand MPMF can benefit from the prestige and credibility of the institutional brand and its long history (i.e., the MPF). Therefore, any image change will have to be included in an effort to change the institutional brand, because when there is similarity between the entity and the brand, it is likely that clients will infer certain similar associations with the brand. Thus, the development of activities defined to modify the institutional image of the MPMF may be consubstantiated in the context of an elitist institution image, through the enlargement of its attraction in the community, and the definition of a program specifically oriented to it, or a partnership program with it that leads small groups of musicians to schools, churches or civic organizations to perform and discuss their music.

Throughout its existence, the MPF has resorted mainly to advertising the event, essentially through: 1) advertisements in several national and local newspapers, as well as in international and national music magazines; 2) advertising spots on national and local radio stations; 3) some spots on the public television channel; 4) posters at the localities where the concerts are taking place and in some neighbouring towns, and the distribution of posters to Portuguese Tourism Centres and travel agencies; and 5) distribution of leaflets and complete programs of the festival.

In the ambit of this policy, we suggest the use of other communication activities to promote the event:

(i) Advertising

In order to reach the objectives that were mentioned (in terms of communication and marketing), certain advertising actions can be developed, choosing several communication forms:

- Due to their geographical selection and their close relationship with the audiences, the regional press and radio stations should play a key role. The present policy of using these media should be reinforced and intensified. On the other hand, the speciality press should also be part of the media plan. Considering the MPMF reference market and the costs associated with each of the communication activities, the national press and radio stations, despite their broadcasting coverage, should play a minor role;
- Outdoor advertising should also be favoured, due to the great visibility and selectivity in geographical terms;
- A way of attracting the young population is by choosing forms of communication used by them. For example, advertisements in the cinemas, at the university, in the city bars, in the shopping centre, at speciality shops, among others; and
- The use of alternative forms of advertising, such as advertising in the ATMs, mobile advertising (on town buses, for instance).

(ii) Public relations

The available means to promote the image and influence the market in the public relations area are also diverse. Thus, at this level we would suggest actions such as:

- Distribution of press releases to all the press, with news directly or indirectly related to the events;
- The development of activities, such as workshops and seminars, before and after the musical performances, in order for the audiences to become more familiar and comfortable with the program;
- Publication and offer of small books that approach, in a simple and pleasant way, themes related to music;
- Strengthening of the relationships with the local community, increasing the organization credibility, so that the product surpasses the cultural limits and embraces a social dimension; and
- To organize regular tours or visits to the Palace facilities for relevant audiences, such as journalists, critics, local authorities and local personalities, among others;

- To provide a crèche (with professional staff) for certain events, in order to encourage family attendance and to work as a relevant distinguishing factor[6].

(iii)Sales promotions and merchandising
To establish a set of incentives with the direct purpose of making people participate and attend events, the following techniques could be used:
- The promotion of series of tickets, with campaigns such as "four for the price of three";
- Price reductions for people willing to buy their tickets in advance (before the beginning of the event);
- The promotion of special prices, such as coupons and other forms of discount;
- Joint promotions: with partnership entities or sponsors of the MPF, the granting of discounts for concerts associated with the purchase of certain products (wines, sweets or jams, for instance), and with visits to the Palace;
- The offer of a ticket to a member of a family or group that visits the Mateus Palace;
- Discounts according to age (for example, 50 years of age is equivalent to 50% discount), at special times and for specific concerts; and
- The creation of a product line (for example, a set of china with the foundation or the festival logotype), as a way of increasing revenues.

(iv) Direct marketing
The use of direct marketing techniques implies the development of a database that concentrates all the necessary information to make a contact, and is an indispensable tool to provide a more specialized communication. The MPF does not have such a database, nor does it use any direct marketing technique. Therefore, we suggest the following actions in order to obtain some information on its public:
- To have a place where the public may express their opinions, complaints, suggestions, satisfaction level (where there would be questions about their identification); to offer a ticket in exchange for the giving of information about the client or to resort to the databases of similar organizations;
- By using that database, mailing could be sent to the clients, containing information on the organization and its activities, on the program, on discounts and incentives; and

- Creation of a webpage: As a form of communication, the internet allows organizations to show their products and services, interacting with the public in a more complete way. It is also an important source for gathering information.

Final remarks

The marketing strategies and tools are perfectly suitable for the performing arts organizations in general and for those that promote music festivals in particular, as long as they take a conscious decision about their needs and the coming benefits. The fast rhythm of changes and the presence of new technologies that bring people together and create relationships, tend to revolutionize the traditional market intervention models. Therefore, the organizations of this sector need to react in order to follow these changes. First of all, it is necessary to change the perspective of management of these organizations, focusing on the real purpose of their art: communication with the audiences. Marketing is one of several excellent tools to accomplish that purpose.

When we think of a music festival as an artistic/cultural product, apart from the need to increase its visibility by creating a good image and using promotion strategies, it is necessary to attract a considerable number of spectators and to maintain the current followers. For that purpose it is necessary to analyse the market and to know its preferences, expectations, interests and intentions, and eventually to create groups of consumers with similar behaviour patterns, adapting the offer to each group, through different actions according to the group's specific characteristic.

The MPF, in the development of its activities related to the organization of the MPMF, has been playing an important role in terms of the reinforcement of regional identity and cohesion, in promoting the region and its cultural heritage, in forming tastes and in the "democratization" of culture in a broad area in serious need of cultural events (Cristóvão *et al.*, 2004). However, its survival and sustainability is, increasingly, related to recognition of the need for a pro-active attitude towards the market, and through the creation of strategies capable of attracting external funding and the consolidation and reinforcement of its own revenues.

Generally, we conclude that the MPF has not been taking full advantage of the available marketing techniques and tools. As we have seen from the marketing practices used, the MPF tends to see marketing only as a synonym of an event's promotion, neglecting other essential components of this management area, such as market research and marketing planning. The reasons for this attitude may be related to factors such as the reduced budget available, or because of a lack of specialized human resources. However, the MPF understands the need to reverse this situation, and the studies of Cristovão *et al.* (2003, 2004) are a point of departure to promote changes in the way the MPF approaches marketing and its potential for the development of audiences.

The results of this work have to be seen in the light of its limitations, given that it is only a case study, which cannot be generalized. In addition, considering that performing arts marketing in Portugal is still in a very incipient phase of development, we acknowledge that there is space for development in this research field. In concrete terms, some ideas for future studies are: the analysis of the importance of marketing planning for the sector's organizations; the study of the perceptions of those promoting music festivals about this area of management; and the use they make of research as a means of obtaining information about the market.

Notes

1   The present article results from the combination of two investigations, carried out by a multidisciplinary team of the University of Trás-os-Montes and Alto Douro (UTAD) of this music Festival (Cristóvão *et al.*, 2003, 2004).

2   In both studies, the individuals were chosen according to a subjective process, from a convenience sampling.

3   This is the segment of potential clients. It is composed by new clients/users of the service, buyer/users of competition products, and individuals that have already participated in events of the festival but who, at the moment when the inquiry was taking place, did not participate.

4   Based on the profile characterization of the public that participated in the festival — 2003 season — we could notice that: the frequent clients are related to the individuals belonging to older age groups with a high education level and higher income rates than the average; and the occasional clients are related to age groups from

31–40 and 41–50 years of age (Cristóvão *et al.*, 2003). It is therefore relevant to pay more attention to these groups of clients.

5 Similarly, in the non-participants analysis, we noticed the association between individuals who do not know the festival and the younger age groups (Cristóvão *et al.*, 2004).

6 This is a very important factor for the attraction of the segment of couples with children (minors) that does not implicate high expenses for the organization.

References

Allen, J., O'Toole, W., McDonnell, I. and Harris, R. (2003) *Organização e Gestão de Eventos*. Rio de Janeiro: Editora Campus, 3™ edição.

Brochand, B., Lendrevie, J., Rodrigues, J.V. and Dionísio, P. (1999) *Publicitor*. Lisboa: Publicaçies Dom Quixote.

Crealey, M. (2003) 'Applying new product development models to the performing arts: Strategies for managing risk', *International Journal of Arts Management* 5(3): pp. 24–33.

Cristóvão, A. (Coord.) Baptista, A., Rodrigues, A.P., Rebelo, J., Correia, L. and Lourenço, L. (2003) *Relatório do Estudo de Avaliação dos Impactes do Festival de Música da Casa de Mateus — uma viagem deslumbrante*. CETRAD, UTAD/DESG, Vila Real.

Cristóvão, A. (Coord.) Baptista, A., Rodrigues, A.P., Rebelo, J., Correia, L. and Lourenço, L. (2004) *Relatório Final do Estudo 2 sobre o Festival de Música na Região do Norte*. CETRAD, UTAD/DESG, Vila Real.

Colbert, F. (2003) 'Entrepreneurship and leadership in marketing the arts', *International Journal of Arts Management* 6(1): pp. 30–39.

Dawson, W.M. (1980) 'The arts and marketing', in Mokwa, M.P., Dawson, W.D. and Prieve, E.A. (eds) *Marketing the arts*. Praeger Publishers: pp. 7–13.

Fillis, I. (2004) 'The entrepreneurial artist as marketer: Drawing from the smaller-firm literature', *International Journal of Arts Management*, 7(1): pp. 9–21.

Frey, B.S. (2003) 'Festivals', in Towse, R. (ed) *A handbook of cultural economics*. Edward Elgar Publishing Limited: pp. 232–235.

Gainer, B. (1989) 'The business of high culture: Marketing the performing arts in Canada', *The Services Industries Journal*, 9 (4): pp. 143–161.

Kotler, P. (1980) 'Foreword', in Mokwa, M.P., Dawson, W.D. and Prieve, E.A. (eds) *Marketing the arts*. Praeger Publishers: pp. xiii–xv.

Kotler, P. (2000) *Marketing para o Século XXI*. Lisboa: Editorial Presença.

Kotler, P. and Armstrong, G. (1993) *Princípios de Marketing*. Rio de Janeiro: Prentice-Hall do Brasil.

Kotler, P. and Levy, S. (1969) 'Broadening the concept of marketing', *Journal of Marketing*, 33: pp. 10–15.

Laczniak, G.R. (1980) 'Product management and the performing arts', in Mokwa, M.P., Dawson, W.D. and Prieve, E.A. (eds) *Marketing the Arts*. Praeger Publishers: pp. 124–138.

Lovelock, C. and Hyde, P. (1980) 'Pricing policies for arts organizations: Issues and inputs', in Mokwa, M.P., Dawson, W.D. and Prieve, E.A. (eds) *Marketing the Arts*. Praeger Publishers: pp. 240–262.

McDonald, H. and Harrison, P. (2002) 'The marketing and public relations practices of Australian performing arts presenters', *International Journal of Nonprofit and Voluntary Sector Marketing* 7(2): pp. 105–117.

Mejon, J.C., Fransi, E.C. and Johansson, A.T. (2004) 'Marketing management in cultural organizations: A case study of Catalan Museums', *International Journal of Arts Management*, 6 (2): pp. 11–22.

Mokwa, M.P., Nakamoto, K. and Enis, B.M. (1980) 'Marketing management and the arts', in Mokwa, M.P., Dawson, W.D. and Prieve, E.A. (eds) *Marketing the Arts*. Praeger Publishers: pp. 14–28.

Petkus Jr, E. (2004) 'Enhancing the application of experiential marketing in the arts', *International Journal of Nonprofit and Voluntary Sector Marketing*, 9(1): pp. 49–56.

Rentschler, R., Radbourne, J., Carr, R. and Richard, J. (2002) 'Relationship marketing, audience retention and performing arts organisation viability', *International Journal of Nonprofit and Voluntary Sector Marketing* 7(2): pp. 118–130.

Scheff, J. and Kotler, P. (1996) 'Crisis in the arts: The marketing response', *California Management Review* 39 (1): pp. 28–52.

Strang, R.A. and Gutman, J. (1980) 'Promotion policy making in the arts: A conceptual framework', in Mokwa, M.P., Dawson, W.D. and Prieve, E.A. (eds) *Marketing the arts*. Praeger Publishers: pp. 225–239.

Yin, R. (1984) *The case study research: Design and methods*. Beverley Hills: Sage.

DRAGONS ON THE WATER: THE INFLUENCE OF CULTURE IN THE COMPETITIVE ADVANTAGE OF TOURISM DESTINATIONS

Pedro Moreira*

Institute For Tourism Studies, Macau SAR, PR China

An old legend...

In a turbulent period of Chinese history, around 2300 years ago, Qu Yuan, a man of wisdom and integrity, was a member of a Chinese feudal kingdom government. Qu Yuan advocated political reforms and due to disagreements with the king and to the manoeuvres of his rivals was considered a traitor and exiled. Dedicating his last years to writing poetry about his people and his country, he was finally defeated by sorrow and drowned in the Bo Luo River, in the Hu-Nan province of China. The fishermen tried to recover his body and jumped into the boats racing to search for him. While they were looking in the waters of the river for the body of Qu Yuan, offers of rice were given to the fish to spare the poet.

The races in dragon shape boats revive the fifth day of the fifth lunar month of the Chinese calendar of 278 B.C. That day, the date when Qu Yuan jumped into the river, is still remembered by the Dragon Boat Festival, celebrating his patriotism. Accounting for the historical importance of the date, in Hong Kong and Macau the corresponding day of the Gregorian calendar is a public holiday.

Introduction

"Tourism (…) is a culture construct, fashioned by the behaviour and customs of each society." Smith and Brent (1991: p. 7)

"(…) new ventures occur in the tourism circuits where explorers in the late twentieth century are willing to buy not only the products but also the experience of life in all its exotic splendour." Nash (2000, p. 129)

In line with the argument that special events are the core of many tourism destinations' promotional strategies (Sofield and Sivan, 2003), this study uses the Macau Dragon Boat Festival as a point of departure to discuss the evolution of festivals and other events originally rooted in traditional culture as destinations develop their tourism industry. It is argued that: (1) the popularity that events like the Dragon Boat Festival might achieve among tourists and residents represents a value of authenticity that is missing in events that are fundamentally produced for tourism consumption, and that (2) the value of authenticity, supported by the active participation of the residents in events that became through time a natural part of their lives, might have long term repercussions in the sustainable development of tourism destinations.

Even when the main reason to visit a tourism destination is not the attendance to a cultural or sport event, there is some evidence that specific visitor segments show interest in these holiday experiences. Moufakkir, Singh, Woud and Holecek (2004) in a study of market seg-mentation of gaming visitors in a casino destination found that 53% of the visitors were not involved in any other activities besides casino gaming and that only very low percentages were planning to attend a sporting event (5%) or a festival (1%). The percentages were, however, significantly different when the three visitor segments were compared, meaning that although the main reason for the trip was generally visiting the casino, the high spenders participated in these two other recreational activities more than the medium or the light spender segments.

The idea that competitive advantages are based on facilities, resorts, hotels, attractions, culture and heritage, service orientation or friendliness of the residents is not so clear anymore as these factors no longer differentiate tourism destinations (Morgan and Pritchard, 2002:

p. 11). Such solutions have been so over utilised that now, instead of creating differentiation they have progressively converted former competitive advantages into competitive standards, raising the level of customers' expectations and producing some other interesting side effects. From a management or organisational theory perspective it seems indeed interesting that in very far away places an almost exact copy of the facilities and services are made available, to a level of detail that can be considered an organisational triumph. At least in principle, it seems doubtful that for tourists, this fact receives such interest. If it is true that a part of the services are generally expected to be available within an universal range, the tourism experience is always expected to be unique, authentic, emotional and memorable, even if it was deliberately designed to produce those effects.

The evolution of a destination's culture under the influence of a society too sensitive to the market's ephemeral variations may alter or destroy forever some of its most unique events. The concept of commodification, describing a phenomenon that involves the development of cultural products designed specifically to attract tourists seeking authentic experiences (Goulding, 2000) in a submission of the original value to the exchange value (Gotham, 2002), represents a real threat of cultural decline to tourism destinations.

The solid links that exist between tourism and culture however do not necessarily mean that culture must be sacrificed to economic progress under a narrow, submissive or deterministic perspective. As an example beyond that approach, events that were once interrupted may be recovered to their original form and even assume a new level of importance due to historical research and investments made possible by the tourism sector decisions and resources. The tourists' interest in cultural aspects of destinations can contribute to rescue at least part of the cultural heritage (Nash, 2000) threatened by the erosion of progress and by the natural development of the modern societies. If a culture evolves exclusively in response to market demands, its values, meanings and original forms may be lost forever. With this loss, one of the competitive advantages that are more difficult to replace or replicate — an advantage based on time, on the accumulation of a singular past — will disappear, along with the differentiation and the competitive advantage of one destination over other rival destinations that are competing for the same market.

What makes one city different from another is its specific culture, the values and beliefs of its citizens and the special experiences that fulfil the tourists' expectations and stimulate their emotions. Events are clearly a part of the social, economic and cultural development of a destination (Pugh and Wood, 2004; Lade and Jackson, 2004) and culture and event tourism can be considered key differentiators for tourism (Lade and Jackson, 2004) generating powerful attractors that are central to the competitive success of a destination. However, as was noted, the efforts to attract more and more visitors might mean the solid and progressive destruction of the destination, leading in consequence to the elimination of an important part of its competitive advantage.

Tourism attractions as systems and the importance of non-material culture

Leiper (1990) extracts a definition of tourism attraction from previous works (MacCannell, 1976; Gunn, 1972; Angyal, 1969; all referred by Leiper, 1990) as a system comprising the tourist (human element), a nucleus (central element), and a marker (informative element). The marker, defined as the information that links the human and the central element, provides perhaps the most important argument in favour of the cultural predominance of attractions like festivals and events, even when compared with material forms of cultural expression, like historical heritage. It is undeniable that historical heritage and monuments represent a cultural legacy but cultural events and festivals are live culture.

In modern tourism, visits to monuments seem to have initially conquered a solid position as valid reasons for travelling. When Thomas Cook, one of the precursors of mass tourism, organised his first commercial trip in July 25, 1845, he presented a list of points of interest that included more than 70 locations and monuments to be visited in the city of Liverpool (Cook, 2000). One factor that might have been important in this first preference of tourism for monuments is the higher time and space stability when compared with events. Whilst monuments are stable in space and over time, events are concentrated in a limited period of time and have a weaker association with a restricted space. These characteristics can, however, be highly positive since: (1) in terms of *time*, events are more flexible and their power of attraction can increase visitor arrivals in low periods; (2) in terms of *space*, events are also more flexible and the decisions on the dedicated locations can respond effectively to destination management and junctural evolution.

The Dragon Boat Race Festival can be considered as a contribution of the Chinese culture to the world culture. It is the most prestigious Chinese Festival in Western countries, capable of attracting over 100,000 spectators as in the World Championship in Vancouver in 1996 (Zauhar, 2004). From a traditional festival in China, the dragon boat races gradually developed as a sport outside the Chinese borders and in 2005 the International Dragon Boat Federation represented 62 member countries and associations. The strong visual appeal of the dragon boats has also been used in marketing for international products and services.

More than a celebration of culture, the races involve a natural sports component. There are references to the link of sports and culture in the case of the Hong Kong Dragon Boat Festival (Zauhar, 2004, Sofield and Sivan, 1994) and according to Zauhar (2004), the dragon boat races can be considered a sport tourism event. When we talk about sports tourism, the sports must be a source of travelling or the main reason to travel, generating an important increase of arrivals. In the case of Macau's festival, there is a dominance of the residents and only a small number of international athletes and visitors travelling to the city primarily to participate or attend the dragon boat races. Nevertheless, tourists that did not come specifically for the dragon boat festival participate in it and it is likely that this will be one of the positive and memorable moments of their stay. In different and special circumstances, world sport events can produce international arrivals that are significantly larger than the resident population (Stovall, 2002). In contrast to special events that attract by themselves massive numbers of visitors for a very specific period of time, when sports are not the central attraction of a tourism destination they can still occupy a supportive position as a retention factor (Zauhar, 2004) or be managed as a secondary or special source of attraction in periods of lower arrivals. Finally, the fact that the dragon boat festival has deep links with the traditional culture may even become more important in the future as the cultural component of tourist experiences and the niche of cultural tourism has been considered an emergent phase in tourism development (Craik, 1997).

On development challenges and dilemmas: A destination meets its destiny or creates a better future

Events that meet tourists and residents expectations represent an ideal balance by contrast with the recurrent supremacy of trade-off decisions that sacrifice the residents' interests to the economic inputs of tourism development. The evolution of cultural attractions is a part of the cycle of evolution of a tourism destination (Butler, 1980) and, as Pugh and Wood note, "urban tourism is now well established and often includes the use of urban settings and city spaces for special events to add value to the overall package offered by the destination" (2004: p. 64). The evolution from a competition between countries to a competition between cities seems clear:

> Global tourism activity has shown a growth of 7.1%/year, from 25 million arrivals in 1950 to 612 million arrivals in 1998. Subsequently, international tourist arrivals are expected to mature, reaching 1.6 billion in 2020 (WTO, 1997a). This trend propels each city worldwide into a competitive situation, necessitating these cities to be providers of tourism services. (Suh and McAvoy, 2005: p. 325)

Tourism is becoming progressively a tourism of cities. To safeguard that the citizens remain interested in living in a city and that the visitors remain interested in visiting and returning to that city one possible solution is the development of a diversified, wide range calendar of events addressed to an also wide range of target markets. A rich and diversified calendar will include events especially directed to tourists or to differentiated segments of tourists considered as specific targets and general interest events that will also appeal to the citizens. Events that are founded on culture, history and tradition have a potential to hold this double appeal, to the citizens due to matters of pride and identity and to the tourists as a way to participate in the "real life" of the city where they are staying.

   In the case of the dragon boat races, in contrast to events and festivals that are directed to specific segments of the tourism market, a single event concentrates the interest of a wide diversity of individuals. That diversity seems to include nationality and demographic diversities and a diversity of cultural and educational backgrounds, as well as professional and economic diversities. Very different people gather to watch the races and shout for the teams that, on the water, face fierce competition for the first places. These differences reflect first of all a strong community support, a key success factor for festival type events (Mayfield and Crompton, 1995; Lade and Jackson, 2004) and are a part of the explanation for the races' success amongst both visitors and residents that may be due to the complementarity of the experience offered to both groups (Figure 1).

There is an underlying assumption that individuals with different cultural backgrounds differ in their experiences of an environment (Kaplan and Kaplan, 1980, referred by Bonn, Joseph and Dai, 2005) and

Figure 1   Some of the reasons why the Dragon Boat Festival attracts both residents and visitors

The residents attend the races because …	**For the visitors the races offer an opportunity to…**
Most of the teams represent local government bureaus, private companies and other groups and organisations and a component of rivalry and competition between the groups is always present. The dragon boat teams are big and the families, friends and colleagues of the teams' members join the competition and spend the racing days around the lake, a beautiful site that, in the same way as the Dragon Boat Festival, offers a pleasant view of a harmonious landscape of the past and the present.	Experience the local culture in a natural, interactive and direct approach, often not available in other cultural events, museums or exhibitions, in which a "don't touch" formal approach still prevails. Contact with the residents, in a very open and positive festival environment.

recent results, in line with past research (Berlyne, 1977; Britton, 1979; Buck, 1977; Thurot and Thurot, 1983, all referred by Bonn, Joseph, Dai, 2005), indicate that differences in cultural backgrounds may lead to differences in destination image perceptions. Hypothetically, the argument can be extended to the perception of a specific event, which again highlights by contrast the general interest that the dragon boat festival receives from a wide diversity of groups. One explanation that might be suggested is the possibility that the different perceptions and experiences of the different groups are positive and compatible, in that the same event offers something interesting, although different, to a wide range of persons.

The development of festivals and events share the general tourism dilemmas of two very different futures involving strategic options about:

- the quality and the authenticity of the experiences *versus* the focus on numbers and the artificiality of the experiences; and
- strengthening the links between the past and the present as culture, history and tradition are kept alive and protected as a legacy to the new generations *versus* a rupture of the links between the past and the present as the values of culture, history and tradition are lost or replaced by economic values.

Instead of advocating extreme choices between the options maybe it could be questioned if a combination of the apparently antagonistic cultural and economic interests is possible and if it can generate positive results. There are interesting signs towards this possibility:

> Although cultural tourism has been promoted largely for its economic benefits, it is now increasingly recognised that cultural tourism can also directly impact on the cultures that tourist come to see. It has been argued that cultural tourism can play a role in helping to preserve cultural traditions. Grahn's (1991) analysis of cultural tourism development in Lapland indicates that cultural tourism can play a positive role in enhancing traditional culture (…). (Richards, 1994: p. 110)

The deterministic view of tourism development seems however to have so far more supporters and more evidence by its side and to be, in a way, more realistic. MacCannell (2001) presents the impact of tourism on a destination's culture in the following way:

The erosion of the specificity of tourism destinations in favour of a homogeneous culture of tourism is the result of the transformation of local economies (…) and also of the movement and displacement of millions of natural historical and cultural objects, including the things that tourists once had to travel to see. (p. 384)

(…) international tourism is vulnerable as a result of its own previous success and excess. When the culture of tourism succeeds in replacing local culture, it becomes increasingly difficult to distinguish between destinations. (p. 388)

There is a two phase impact of tourism on the original culture. First the original culture is modified or replaced by a tourism enhancing culture. As this new culture becomes dominant the initial cultural uniqueness that might have been an origin of competitive advantage gradually disappears, leading to the fading of the attraction and to the disappearance of the competitive strength of the event or destination. Sofield and Sivan (2003: pp. 9–10) mention that the evolution of the Hong Kong dragon boat festival was influenced by tourism in this way:

Originally one component in a year-long cycle of rituals centred around Tin Hau, the Goddess of the Sea, to protect Chinese fishing communities and ensure their future prosperity, the Tuen Ng under the impact of development and marketing for tourism has become a very different event. In anthropological terms it has moved from the sacred to the profane.

The natural evolution of events seems to share the "curse" of tourism destinations synthesised by Butler (1980: p. 6):

Destination areas carry with them the potential seeds of their own destruction, as they allow themselves to become more commercialized and loose their qualities (…).

(…) there seems to be overwhelming evidence that the general pattern of tourist area evolution is consistent. The rates of growth and change may vary widely, but the final result will be the same in almost all cases.

Although there are exceptions, this change process seems to be inevitable even if there are efforts towards sustainable development (Butler, 1997).

Since the evolution of culture is inexorable, there are at least two strategic challenges that should be considered in this area. The first of these challenges seems to be the management of the speed of the process of culture change, in order to protect the cultural assets and delay as long as possible the destruction of the nucleus of the competitive advantage. A second challenge is the management of the "shape" of the general evolution of the destinations' culture, to highlight the strategic priorities, what should be protected and how these aspects of culture should be preserved, strengthened and presented as factors of tourism attraction. Both challenges are critical to the protection of the cultural uniqueness of a destination, a uniqueness that may represent a solid element in its competitive advantage.

Discussion

The over development of a tourism attraction, a festival or an event can destroy the authenticity and the quality of the traveller's experience. However, it is not inevitable that the economic progress and the evolution of a destination must involve the total sacrifice of its culture. Better alternatives can be found in the direction of a more graceful and balanced line of growth but, as mentioned by Timothy and Prideaux (2004), societies are vulnerable to a strong temptation to commercialise their heritage and their culture.

The debate on the trade off between the economic yields and the negative cultural impacts of tourism seems far from over, not only in terms of festivals and events, but in the totality of the tourism product. A solution of compromise seems for now the only realistic one since the extreme solutions of the full sacrifice of cultural authenticity to financial revenues may not have means to resist in the long term to the emergence of opportunistic copycat competitors, and the full sacrifice of the economic incomes, besides being utopian, would probably lead to a gradual degradation of culture due to the lack of interest and the insufficiency of resources.

The changes produced by tourism in the original characteristics of destinations, even within a philosophy of sustainable development, and the reliance of tourism development upon artificial and culturally empty attractions generates a high vulnerability since such competitive advantages can be replicated and developed elsewhere (Butler, 1997). As

Carter and Beeton (2004) argue, there is a trade-off between residents and tourists involving cultural economic expressions and economic benefits. The cultural and economic exchanges are evidence that culture is not only something that attracts tourists but more, that it has an economic value. Of course, as with other products there is a difference of value and price between the originals and the copies, what is genuine and what is counterfeit.

In the case of Macau, the Dragon Boat Festival has been progressively developing into one of the most meaningful events of the Macau calendar. The dragon boats, as the Mid Autumn Festival lanterns and moon cakes and the red packets of the Chinese New Year (Siu, 2001), bring the old and the new together, the tradition and the culture of the past to our present life, with a true meaning that contrasts with more empty and artificial event formats created specifically to attract tourists. The cultural authenticity of the Macau Dragon Boat Festival can be confirmed by several factors: (1) the historical roots of the festival; (2) the regularity of this "social ritual" and the natural participation of the citizens; (3) the political recognition of the importance of the festival as one of the holidays of the city's official calendar; (4) the strong linkage between the dragon boat teams and the staff of public or private organisations integrated in the economic and social mosaic; (5) the secondary plan of the direct economic value of the festival, showing a generally rare precedent of tradition over economic interests. Events with a strong cultural component such as the Dragon Boat Festival might generate low direct economic revenues and hold therefore a reduced viability in a standalone mode but when considered integrated in the overall calendar of a destination, contribute to its competitiveness and thus indirectly to its economic performance. Furthermore, the importance of such events in the preservation of the lifestyle of the residents of tourism destinations represents in addition a positive value to the protection of the cultural authenticity and to the necessary balance required for long term sustainable development.

Indeed, a stronger competitive advantage is one in which the core differentiation and authenticity are built by history and time, one that is supported by a real meaning and therefore, much more difficult or even impossible to replicate. Of course there is the argument that only a small number of tourists are prepared to notice the difference and that an even smaller number thinks that this difference is important. The really different results of the two approaches only become evident in the long term. The long term however, is generally obfuscated by the more immediate economic interests, seems very far away in the future, and is therefore often treated as irrelevant. Well, once upon a time, a long time ago in a very distant place there was a white goose that one day laid a golden egg...

References

Bonn, M., Joseph, S., Dai, M. (2005) 'International versus domestic visitors: An examination of destination image perceptions', *Journal of Travel Research* Vol. 43, February: pp. 294–301.

Butler, R. (1980) 'The concept of a tourist area cycle of evolution: Implications for management of resources', *Canadian Geographer* Vol. 24, No. 1: pp. 5–12.

Butler, R. (1997) 'Modelling tourism development: Evolution, growth and decline', in S. Wahab, J. Pigram (eds), *Tourism, development and growth: The challenge of sustainability*, London: Routledge, pp. 109–125.

Carter, R., Beeton, R. (2004) *A model of cultural change and tourism*. Asia Pacific Journal of Tourism Research Vol. 9, No. 4: pp. 423–442.

Cook. T. (2000) *A hand book of the trip from Leicester, Nottingham, and Derby to Liverpool and the Coast of North Wales*. London: Routledge.

Gotham, K. (2002) 'Marketing Mardi Gras: Commodification, spectacle and the political economy of tourism in New Orleans', *Urban Studies* Vol. 39, No. 10, pp. 1735–1756.

Goulding, C. (2000) 'The commodification of the past, postmodern pastiche, and the search for authentic experiences at contemporary heritage attractions', *European Journal of Marketing* Vol. 34, No. 7, pp. 835–853.

Lade, C., Jackson, J. (2004) 'Key success factors in regional festivals: Some Australian experiences', *Event Management* Vol. 9: pp. 1–11.

Leiper, N. (1990) 'Tourism attraction systems', *Annals of Tourism Research* Vol. 17, No. 2: pp. 367–384.

MacCannell, D. (2001) 'Remarks on the commodification of cultures', in V. Smith and M. Brent (eds) *Hosts and guests revisited: Tourism issues of the 21st century*. New York: Cognizant, pp. 380–390

Mayfield, T., Crompton, J. (1995) 'The status of the marketing concept among festival organisers', *Journal of Marketing* Vol. 54: pp. 20–35.

Morgan, N. Pritchard, A., Pride, R. (2002) *Destination branding: Creating the unique destination position.* Oxford: Butterworth Heinemann.

Moufakkir, O., Singh, A., Woud, A., Holecek, D. (2004) 'Impact of light, medium and heavy spenders on casino destinations: Segmenting gaming visitors based on amount of non-gaming expenditures', *Gaming Research and Review Journal* Vol. 8, No. 1: pp. 59–71.

Nash, J. (2000) 'Global integration and the commodification of culture', *Ethnology* Vol. 39, No. 2: pp. 129–131.

Pugh, C., Wood, E. (2004) 'The strategic use of events within local government: A study of London Borough Councils', *Event Management* Vol. 9: pp. 61–71.

Richards, G. (1994) 'Cultural tourism in Europe', in C. Cooper and A. Lockwood (eds) *Progress in tourism, recreation and hospitality management.* Chichester: John Wiley, pp. 99–115.

Siu, K. (2001) 'Red Packet: A traditional object in the modern world', *Journal of Popular Culture*, vol. 35, No. 3: pp. 103–125.

Smith, V., Brent, M. (2001) 'Introduction', in V. Smith and M. Brent (eds) *Hosts and guest revisited: Tourism issues of the 21st century.* New York: Cognizant, pp. 1–11.

Sofield, T., Sivan, A. (2003) 'From cultural festival to international sport — The Hong Kong dragon boat races', *Journal of Sport Tourism* Vol. 8, No. 1: pp. 9–20.

Stovall, T. (2002) 'Forum French Tourism and Tourists in France — Introduction: Bon Voyage!', *French Historical Studies* Vol. 25, No. 3: pp. 415–422.

Suh, Y., McAvoy, L. (2005) 'Preferences and trip expenditures — a conjoint analysis of visitors to Seoul, Korea', *Tourism Management* Vol. 26: pp. 325–333.

Timothy, D., Prideaux, B. (2004) 'Issues in heritage and culture in the Asia Pacific region', *Asia Pacific Journal of Tourism Research* Vol. 9, No. 3: pp. 213–223.

Zauhar, J. (2004) 'Historical perspectives of sports tourism', *Journal of Sport Tourism* Vol. 9, No.1: pp. 5–101.

RANGE, IMPACT AND INTERACTIONS OF FESTIVALS AND EVENTS IN POZNAN — A CITY OF MUCH MORE THAN JUST INTERNATIONAL TRADE FAIRS: THE DEVELOPMENT OF CULTURAL AND EVENT TOURISM

Karolina Buczkowska

Faculty of Tourism and Recreation, University School of Physical Education in Poznan, Poland

Introduction

All cultures celebrate and the things, persons or themes they value provide reasons for festivals and other special events (Jafari, 2000: p. 226). It has also not been much different over the years in the case of Poznan — a city of more than half a million inhabitants — a cradle of the Polish State, which history dates as far back as the 10th Century and which is primarily known in Europe as a city of international and national trade fairs.

The Poznan International Fairs and consequently the city of Poznan became an institution especially after the Second World War. Every year the event expanded and attracted many visitors. Due to the Fairs' activity, Poznan obtained many economic, political and trade benefits during the last several years. During communism the Fairs used to be 'a window out to the world' and an opportunity for contact with foreigners. Participation in the fairs gave Poles a unique — even though for a short while — feeling of being nearer to Europe, which was closed for them at that time. For foreign visitors the Fairs, in turn, created the possibility of an unproblematic access to Poland in order to make interesting business contacts with the representatives of many countries as well as to visit the incredible city of Poznan. To make the Fairs' events more interesting and to give an opportunity for the Fairs' tourists (both national as well as foreign exhibitors and visitors) to get to know the rich culture and tradition of the city every year numerous cultural, touristic and entertaining events were organized for them. Thanks to that one can say today that the Fairs contributed to the development of the city's cultural life in the post-war period, gradually leading to a real revolution in that area. It can also be said that fair-like Poznan, as it has now been perceived for at least 50 years, is presently one of the centers of Polish (and not only Polish) culture, and the generated cultural and event tourism which emerged as a consequence of the Fairs-related events is treated equally with a rich Poznan trade fair tourism. At present, simultaneously with numerous business and trade events — such as fairs and sales, consumer and trade shows, expositions, meetings, conferences, etc. — all categories of planned events take place in the City area on an annual basis. These are among others:

- cultural celebrations — such as festivals, parades, religious ceremonies, heritage commemoration;
- art and entertainment events — concerts, other performances, exhibits, award ceremonies;
- sport competitions, education and scientific events;
- recreational events — games and sports for fun, amusements;
- political and state occasions — inaugurations, VIP visits, rallies (Jafari, 2000: p. 209).

Fairs tourism vs. cultural celebrations and arts events since post-war times

The origins of contemporary cultural celebrations and art events — as these have been especially connected with the fairs — can be traced back to the first post-war fairs events, especially those organized in Poznan always in June. In 1950 the main fair event known as *Poznan International Fairs* hosted 429 exhibitors from 19 countries and was visited by 1.115 million people, including 1100 foreigners. For all those people the cultural institutions of Poznan organized 157 theatre performances, several concerts of classical and choir music, 200 open-air concerts, and 440 cinema screenings. Additionally, the Opera house inaugurated the fair event with the premiere of one of the plays, which established a continued tradition of the Opera and Trade Fairs for many years to come.

In 1956, in turn, trade fairs, which took part in June, were frequented by 1.234 million people (a record number in the history of Poznan International Fairs), and the number of exhibitors increased to 1550. Five years later, in 1960, the number of people visiting the fairs reached the level of 450 thousand and remained at the same level until the late 1980s. Over the years there has been an increase in the number of foreign trade tourists, reaching the number of 14000 people in 1970 (almost 13 times more than in 1950). Since 1960 the number of trade exhibitors has been increasing, oscillating most often around 3-5 thousand annually (WUS, 1986: p. 94, 95).

Consequently with the development of the main June trade event and the introduction of specialized fairs organized in other months (since 1973), the circle of fairs-related events organizers has gradually been enlarging and the repertoire has been enriched. The richness of the cultural and sight-seeing repertoire organized for the Fairs' guests and tourists (exhibitors and visitors) has added every year to an increasing general attractiveness of the Fairs and consequently, the attractiveness of the city itself. It has also created a possibility to make foreigners and inhabitants of other Polish regions familiar with the cultural and historical richness of Poznan, as well as it has enriched the life of the citizens of Poznan, who often were involved in providing services for numerous undertakings. ·

The event, which is inseparably connected with the main trade fairs is St. John's Fair, taking place annually in June. It is the biggest outdoor event in Poznan, that originated exactly 30 years ago in 1976. The opening of the event on the 5th of June 1976, 2 hours after the commencement of Poznan International Fairs, was a special reference to a mediaeval tradition of June *St. John's contracts*, and the event itself became a background for meetings of merchants, artists, craftsmen as well as tourists. The Fair always lasts about a week and burghers' houses and stalls in the Old Town Market Square are filled with handicrafts, antiques, military accessories and delicacies of Poznan cuisine. Street-musicians and folklore bands can be heard everywhere and theatre performances take place in varied architectural environments. Every year the event is made even more attractive by concerts and shows of known Polish and foreign artists.

The culture of Poznan cannot be discussed without mentioning the importance and enormous merits of music, song and dance in the city and the related events, performed nowadays both in the context of the fairs and also outside it. Among various cyclic music events, which took place in Poznan and which over years became inseparably connected with the fairs were: performance of the Polish Dance Theatre of the Poznan Konrad Drzewiecki Ballet (every year the theatre came back from its national and international tours especially for the main trade events), symphonic concerts of the Poznan Philharmonics and the Polish Radio Chamber Orchestra ("Amadeus") conducted by Agnieszka Duczmal. An inseparable part of the fair events in Poznan was also "The Encounters with Music", which took place in the Town Hall of the Old Market Square. The special attraction of "The Encounters" had always been choir concerts, especially those performed by "The Poznan Nightingales" Boys and Men's Choir conducted by Stefan Stuligrosz and "The Polish Nightingales" Poznan Boys' Choir conducted by Jerzy Kurczewski, and later by Wojciech Krolopp. Furthermore, thanks to the fairs such events as: Fairs' Days of Organ and Chamber Music, Promenade Concerts of Brass Orchestras, National Confrontation of Bagpipers' Folk Groups and Folklore Days, were brought to life.

Contemporary off-fairs events

Political changes which took place in Poland after 1989, the end of communism followed by the birth of democracy and self-government brought about even more involvement of various municipal institutions and several independent associations organizing cultural events, not any more exclusively for the fairs' guests and fairs' tourists, but also for the inhabitants and tourists of cultural tourism and event tourism. Freedom of speech, abandonment of censorship, freedom in contacts with the West initiated in Poznan new, brave and independent events.

One of those turned out to be the "Malta" International Theatre Festival, which has become another — following Poznan Fairs — business card and landmark for the city in Europe. "Malta" was inaugurated in 1991 at the Maltanese Lake shore, immediately after the end of the June fairs. This event has turned Poznan into one big experimental theatre stage and has become one of the most prominent events of its type in Central and Eastern Europe. The Festival is often linked to Scotland's Edinburgh Festival because aside from fringe theatre, the visitors can also view here contemporary dance groups, cult film screenings, photo exhibitions and abstract art. From year to year the Festival has attracted more and more theatres and public from all over the world. During the first "Malta" in 1991 ten performances were presented by 6 theater groups from the 3 countries of: Poland, Italy and Spain. However, at the 10th Festival in the year 2000 the audience was offered in the main program the opportunity to view twenty two performances presented by 8 Polish, 3 French, 2 Spanish groups, and one group from the countries of: Chile, Cuba, Italy, USA and Turkey. Twenty nine groups from Poland, Czech Republic, India, Argentina, Ukraine, Italy and the Netherlands performed in the category *Malta Off.*

Some of the most popular events among the City's inhabitants have, since the 1990s, been those that popularize historical values and traditions of the city. One such event is St. Martin's Day which takes place on the 11th of November, on the calendar name day of Martin. A colourful parade strolls alongside the street of St. Martin, led by 'St. Martin' riding a white horse. The parade stops in front of the Poznan Castle, where various concerts continue. One tradition of that day, which is unique to Poznan, is baking of sweet croissants which, as legend tells, take their shape from the horseshoe worn by the horse on which St. Martin rode into the city many years ago. Another equally interesting event, which always takes place at the end of June, is the so called — City Name day, in other words the Day of City Patrons: St. Peter and Paul. Every year the event is given another theme and is organized in another city point, which makes it attract crowds of people. Traditions and history of the city and its region are cultivated also during such events as Poznan Bethlehem — connected with Christmas, The Bread Festival, The Harvest Day (both events take place at the end of summer), as well as The Poznan Dialect Speaking Contest "Speak Our Way" and Pyrlandia Days [Potato Land Days].

Among events, which are not related to the Fairs and which quickly gained in popularity, special attention must be paid to Biennial and Workshops of Contemporary Dance organized alternatively since 1994 by the Polish Dance Theatre — the Poznan Ballet (connected for many years with the institution of the Poznan International Fairs). Biennial and Workshops always take place in August and are frequented by people of different ages coming to Poznan from all over Poland and Europe. In 1994, 250 people took part in the first biennial which was organized, but due to growing interest in the event in 2004 the organizers were forced to limit the number of participants to 2100 people per year. For 7 days the participants have the opportunity to see dance and dance performances in various sceneries of the city and to practice under the supervision of the world's best dancers and choreographers. The presented and practised dance kinds include: modern, modern jazz, barre au sol, funky jazz, Broadway jazz, Hindu, flamenco, afro dance, step, contact improvisation, choreotherapy, etc. (Jaköbczak, 2001; p. 96–102).

At present, numerous music events, the titles of which speak for themselves, are also organized: The Henryk Wieniawski International Violin Competition (takes place every 5 years since 1952), "Age of Jazz" Festival, Biennial and Workshops of Contemporary Dance, Poznan Musical Spring, PoznaD Ballet Spring Bagpipe Players' Rally, Poznan Mozart Festival, International "Verba Sacra" Festival, Old Music – "Persona Grata", International Festival of Boys' Choirs, International Festival of University Choirs "Universitat Cantat", New Yorker Hip Hop Festival, "Integrations": World Folklore Review, Festival of Passion and Paschal Music.

The city never forgets about its children and youth, and thus apart from the fairs connected with children's fashion or school accessories, very popular Poznan Fair Meetings (e.g. "Books for Children and Young People") are organized annually in May. When discussing events and festivals prepared for the youngest one needs to mention the International Festival of Films for Young Viewers "Ale Kino!" ["What a Cinema!"] the Poznan Review of Small Theatrical Forms and Biennial of Children's Art. Students, however, celebrate annually during Juvenilia Festival — University Student Culture Days.

Numerous contacts made between Polish and foreign companies at the fairs over the years, brought about the twinning of Poznan with several countries (first in 1966 and 1979 and later in the 1990s.) and also in establishing associations of various countries' admirers. At present Poznan cooperates with towns and regions from 11 different countries, among others: Assen in the Netherlands (cooperation developing since 1992), Brno in the Czech Republic (since 1966), Charkov in Ukraine (since 1998), Jyvaskyla in Finland (since 1979), Hanover in Germany (since 1979), Nablus in Palestine (since 1997), Pozuelo de Alarcon in Spain (since 1992), Nottinghamshire County in the UK (since 1994), Rennes in France (since 1998), Shenzen in China (since 1993) and Toledo in Ohio in the USA (since 1991). Among numerous associations in Poznan the activity of a few of them is worth mentioning: Lovers of France, Japan, Ireland, Lvov, Vilnius and its region, Bamberg in Germany, China and Israel. The above mentioned international contacts resulted in (among others) various international events, which aim to provide further entertainment for the inhabitants of Poznan and tourists as well as to familiarize them with the culture, tradition and ceremonies of other nations. These events are also willingly observed by the fairs' guests, still numerously frequenting Poznan in relation to various fairs exhibits. It happens quite often that French exhibitors come to Poznan during ongoing French Culture Days or Brittany Days, the Irish come for the celebration of St. Patrick's Days, the Lithuanians to the so called "Kaziuki" (St.Casimir's Days), the Japanese to the Days of Japanese culture, the Germans to Hoffmann Festival (Polish-German Opera), and all those with Celtic blood in their veins to the International Celtic Festival, and so on. Interest in the culture of other countries and nations developed in Poznan in a measurable way in the 1990s. It was then that Poles for the first time for many years had the freedom of speech within their societies and associations (other than the Workers' Party or the Association of Polish-Russian Friendship) and could freely travel to the countries they have admired for many years.

Cultural and event tourism in Poznan — definitions, covered functions and conditions for development

The development of cultural and special events in Poznan over the years — both in connection with the Fairs and outside them — has brought about a change in the city character from a typically fair oriented city into a city with a great emphasis on culture. Apart from trade tourism (and sight-seeing tourism (not mentioned in this chapter, but existing in the city for decades and connected with visiting objects of historical value and interest from an architectural point of view), cultural tourism started thriving in Poznan. Cultural tourism, which in the times of communism had only a complementary function to trade tourism, became at the beginning of the 1990s a totally independent form of tourism. An expanded programme prepared with tourists in mind as well as many events organized within its range, make the inhabitants of Poznan have the possibility to participate extensively in the performances. When referring to typical tourists coming to town (both national and foreign), the concept of cultural tourism (in relation to those tourists) is understood as:

1. Holiday tourism with a cultural motivation, such as: trips to towns of an artistic and historical value, visits to museums and galleries, tours covered with a goal of attending artistic and other cultural events (Medlik, 1995: p. 81-82).
2. Movements of persons for essentially cultural motivations, such as study tourism, performing arts and cultural tours, travel to festivals and other cultural events, visits to sites and monuments, travel to study nature, folklore or art, and pilgrimages (WTO, 1982, in Evans, 1993).
3. Commercialised manifestation of the human desiring to see how others live; a demand of a curious tourist to see other peoples in their 'authentic' environment and to view the physical manifestations of their lives as expressed in arts and crafts, music, literature, dance, food and drink, play, handicrafts, language and ritual (Dewar, in Jafari, 2000: p. 126).
4. Travelling connected with cultural properties, which comprise among other things: familiarization with new places, societies, cultures; participation in cultural and artistic events as well as interest in art, architecture and history (Janusewicz, 2002: p. 110).
5. Activity of people in places of their touristic destination and while traveling, which allows them to get to know and experience different lifestyles of other people — lifestyles reflecting social customs, religious traditions, intellectual thought, cultural heritage, which are to meet people's needs, wishes and expectations within the range of culture (Studzienicki, 2002: p. 11)

Cultural tourism, which developed in Poznan during the last 55 years, fulfills various functions: tutoring, relaxing, educating, cognitive and similar to trade and sight-seeing tourism also an urbanization function, called also a city generating one. The last one being especially important from an economic and social point of view because it influences the character of the whole city, spatial aspects of urbanization processes, growth of employment, taking advantage of city values, growth of accommodation, gastronomy and trade-service networks. It shapes in an important way the standard of living for the inhabitants. On the other hand, continuous development of a city dictates the pace and the direction of tourism development as well as it contributes to an increased attractiveness for investors (Alejziak, 1999 and Gaworecki, 1994) and — as in the case of Poznan- for the participants of the Fairs. As a result of those relations at present there are several fair events organized annually among which the most important ones are: BUDMA — International Construction Fair; SECUREX — International Security Exibition; INFOSYSTEM — International Fairs of Telecommunication, Information, Technology and Electronics; CHILD'S WORLD — Trade Fairs of Goods for Children; POLIGRAFIA — International Fair of Printing Machines, Material and Services; EUROFOTO — Trade Fair of Photographic Products and Services; EURO-REKLAMA — International Trade Fair of Advertising Goods and Services; POZNAN MOTOR SHOW; SALDENT — International Dentistry Fair; LOOK — Hairdressing and Cosmetics Forum; MEBLE [FURNITURE]– Fair of Furniture, Accessories and Furnishing; DREMA — International Trade Fair of Woodworking Machines and Tools; INNOVATIONS — TECHNOLOGIES — MACHINES POLAND; INVESTFIELD — Real Estate Fair; "NA RYBY" ["LET'S GO FISHING"] — Angling Equipment Trade Fairs; POZNAN FASHION DAYS — Fair of Clothing and Fabrics; POLAGRA-FOOD — International Trade Fair for the Food Industry; POLAGRA-FARM — International Agricultural Trade Fair.

With regard to the advantages that a city generating function gives to culture, in the current year more than 110 offers of the biggest and the most important festivals and other cultural celebrations and art events of the city, contracted by the Department of Culture and Art of the City Hall in Poznan, are evident within *The Calendar of Cultural Events*. Besides those already mentioned, other interesting events are: "May Picnic with a Book", Photography Biennial Exhibition, "Events Worth Knowing" — presentation of the municipal and regional culture, the International Film Festival "Off Cinema" as well as the International Theatre Festival "Masks".

The development of cultural tourism in the city of Poznan has become possible in recent years due to the existing rich networks of hotels, gastronomy (catering), services (including entertainment), which have been created in the city over the years with the Fairs' guests and tourists in mind. Also today the price range of accommodation in Poznan varies accordingly: off-Fairs season, Fairs class B season (of a smaller range) and Fairs class A season (of the highest importance). It might be that the further process of evolution of cultural tourism will make the owners of hotels/accommodation introduce the price lists adjusted to the period 'before and after the "Malta" Theatre Festival or the Wieniawski Violin Contest', etc.

The splitting of trade fair tourism and cultural tourism (inseparable during communism) observed in the recent years has been caused by two main factors. Firstly, the cultural celebrations as well as art and entertainment events attracted a big (national and foreign) audience outside the fairs. Secondly, the self-sufficiency of the Poznan International Fairs Institution to organize entertainment for its guests without the necessity of leaving the fairs' grounds. According to the national results of research carried out since the year 2000 among the fairs' guests by order of the Polish Fairs Corporation, it turned out that the Fairs' offer called *The Fairs Plus* comprising numerous happenings, concerts, contests, shows, is extremely popular. Almost half of the so called visitors-consumers, i.e. typical fair tourists, have declared in the questionnaires that the attendance at fairs is "simply for entertainment, because the fairs have a good programme" (PKT, 2004; p. 2).

Conclusion

Independent from historical processes and political-economic conditions in Poland and all over the world over the years, the range, impacts and interactions occurring between the trade fairs and cultural events and between various organizers and receivers of both were noticeable in Poznan all the time. A well known historian of Poznan, professor Trzeciakowski, said a few years ago that "Had it not been for the Fairs, Poznan would not be the city it is today"; and that "The Fairs Muses have always loved and will continue to love Poznan International Fairs, because for years this institution supported the culture of Poznan" (Trzeciakowski, 1996: p. 98). Trade fair tourism in Poznan has evolved over the years consistent with the observation that "There is no tourism without culture" (WTO, 1995: p. 6), and thanks to the Fairs, real cultural and event tourism, i.e. travel for personal enrichment (Adams, 1995: p. 32) could develop in the city. At present, more than half a century since the birth of the Poznan Fairs, the dominant forms of tourism in the city (national and foreign) — according to the research carried out in 2002 by the Voivodship Center for promotion and Information in Poznan — are sight-seeing and cultural tourism. Trade Fair tourism and business tourism come in third position among foreign tourists and more than fourth position among national tourists (WOPiI, 2002: pp. 1–4). Taking into consideration all the above mentioned arguments, the statement in the title of this paper that Poznan is a city of much more than just international trade fairs, even though it is still perceived so by many, seems to be legitimate.

References

Adams, G. D. (1995) 'Cultural tourism: the arrival of the intelligent traveler', *Museum News*, December: pp. 32–35.

Alejziak, W. (1999) *Turystyka w obliczu wyzwan XXI wieku* [Tourism in the face of challenge of 21st century]. Krakow: ALBIS.

Co dobrego w poznanskiej kulturze [What's good in Poznan cultural life. Events of 2003]. Wydarzenia 2003. Zapowiedzi 2004 [Events of 2003. Announcements for 2004] (2004). Poznan: Wydawnictwo Miejskie.

Czubinski, A. (1999) 'Miedzynarodowe Targi Poznanskie w okresie powojennym 1945-1996' ['Poznan International Fairs in the post-war period 1945-1996'], *Kronika miasta Poznania — Miedzynarodowe Targi Poznanskie* (special issue). Poznan: Wydawnictwo Miejskie, pp. 172–185.

Evans, G. L. (1993) *Arts and cultural tourism in Europe: definitions and markets,* 2nd International Arts Management Conference. Paris: Groupe HEC.

Gaworecki, W. (1994) *Turystyka* [Tourism]. Warszawa: PWE.

Jafari, J. (ed) (2000) *Encyclopedia of tourism.* London: Routledge.

Janusiewicz, A. (2002) 'Dziedzictwo kulturowe w turystyce polskiej' ['Cultural heritage in the tourism of Poland'], *Problemy turystyki,* No. 1–2: pp. 105–117.

Lobozewicz, T. and G. Binczyk (2001) *Podstawy turystyki* [The basis of tourism]. Warszawa: Wyzsza Szkola Ekonomiczna.

Materialy promocyjne dotyczace miasta Poznania [promotional materials concerning Poznan].

Materialy dotyczace Festiwalu Teatralnego "Malta" [materials concernig "Malta" International Theatre Festival.]

Medlik, S. (1995) *Leksykon podrozy, turystyki, hotelarstwa* [Lexicon of Travel, tourism and hotel industry]. Warszawa: Wyd. Naukowe PWN.

Poznan i jego miasta partnerskie [Poznan and its twin-towns] (2000). Poznan: Wydawnictwo Miejskie.

Poznan 1946–1985 (etc — WUS) (1986). Poznan: Wielkopolski Urzad Statystyczny.

Poznan International Fair 2005 (2005). Poznan: Poznan International Fair.

Prezentacja badan Polskiej Korporacji Targowej (PKT) w ramach programu badawczego Miedzynarodowego Zwiazku Statystyk Targowych CENTREX [The Poland Fair Corporation (PKT) research presentation within the confines of Fair Statistics International Association CENTREX] (2004). Poznan: PKT.

Ruch turystyczny przyjazdowy do Poznania turystow z kraju i zagranicy w letnim sezonie turystycznym 2002 [National and international arrival tourism in Poznan in summer touristic period 2002] — wyniki badan Wielkopolskiego Osrodka Promocji i Informacji w Poznaniu WOPiI (2003). Poznan: WOPiI.

Studzienicki, T. (2002) 'Turystyka kulturowa jako element polityki turystycznej regionu' ['Cultural tourism as an element of region tourism policy'], *Problemy Turystyki i Hotelarstwa*, No. 4: pp. 11–16.

The Calendar of Cultural Events (2004). Poznan: the Department of Culture and Art of the City Hall w Poznaniu.

—— (2005). Poznan: the Department of Culture and Art of the City Hall w Poznaniu.

Trzeciakowski, L. (ed) (1996) *Z biegiem lat. 75 lat Miedzynarodowych Targow Poznanskich* [In the course of time. 75 years of Poznan International Fairs]. Poznan: Miedzynarodowe Targi Poznanskie.

Word Tourism Organisation (1995) Report of the Secretary General of the General Programme of the Work for the Period 1984–1985, Madrid: World Tourism Organisation.

RECREATING CHINA IN THE NORTH OF ENGLAND: FORMS AND FUNCTIONS OF CHINESE 'NEW YEAR' FESTIVALS

Philip Long
Centre for Tourism and Cultural Change
Sheffield Hallam University, UK

Xiaoke Sun
School of Tourism, University of Wuhan, China

Introduction

In the United Kingdom, as in many other countries, several cities possess long-established ethnic Chinese communities and, in some cases, designated 'Chinatown' districts. These areas typically include Chinese restaurants, retailers and other community enterprises in streetscapes that incorporate more or less authentically themed Chinese designs and symbols. They are also increasingly being promoted as attractions for tourists, shoppers and new inhabitants of regenerating city centres.

Chinatowns, along with locations elsewhere in British cities, also provide settings for the celebration of Chinese themed festivals and events. The Chinese New Year, or Spring Festival, held around the first day of the first lunar month each year, is the most significant event in Chinese communities' social calendars. At these festivals, community traditions are expressed, renewed, re-interpreted, celebrated and displayed to others through colourful and lively programmes featuring dragon and lion dancing, music, parades and feasting. Unsurprisingly, resident British ethnic Chinese communities play a leading role in the staging of these festivals; alongside more recent and temporary migrants from China and, increasingly, local government professionals from outside the British Chinese community.

This chapter offers an exploratory discussion of Chinese festivals in the UK through brief case studies of York, Manchester and Sheffield. It draws on concepts from the academic literature concerning diaspora communities to suggest some new research directions on this neglected topic.

'Diasporic' community festivals such as Caribbean / Latin American carnivals, St. Patrick's Day celebrations and South Asian Melas have, in recent years, been subject to growing interest from researchers (see, for example Nurse, 2004; 1999). Such festivals are also of interest to policy makers and professionals in economic development, community development, arts, culture and tourism. Typically, these festivals are seen as possessing the potential of encouraging and improving inter-communal dialogue, showcasing community artistic talent, developing positive place images and as a vehicle for tourism promotion. Policy and professional attention is therefore focused on the contribution that diasporic community festivals can make to, for example; social inclusivity, place promotion, identity building and inter-cultural communication.

The chapter is based on a review of literature concerning diaspora communities in general and the Chinese community in the UK in particular. Exploratory interviews were also conducted with representatives of local communities and local government in each of the three cities. Cultural and tourism policy documents for each of the three cities were also scrutinised for content relevant to the development of Chinese community festivals and their connections with wider tourism and cultural policies. Interim findings from this research are presented here.

Diaspora communities and festivals

The concept of diaspora is useful in the analysis of festivals and cultural events that are associated with ethnic minority communities. Diaspora theory combines perspectives from migration studies, globalisation, international relations, sociology and anthropology in explorations of the histories and dynamic natures of ethnic communities worldwide (Axel, 2002; Brubaker, 2005; Coles and Timothy, 2004; Werbner, 2004). The concept therefore offers a basis for exploring diaspora festivals and cultural events through analysis of a community's past and present, as well as from local to global scales. This section offers a brief review of some of the key ideas from the diaspora literature that may usefully be applied to the study of festivals and cultural events.

Diasporic communities are distributed globally, regionally and locally. Ethnic Chinese communities are often concentrated symbolically, if not residentially in Chinatown districts. In the UK, for example ethnic Chinese people are the most widely dispersed community residentially and geographically, reflecting the widespread distribution of takeaway restaurant businesses (Baker, 1994). However, prominent Chinatown districts also exist in a number of British cities. The location of Chinese festivals is likely to mirror this distribution of the community.

Diasporic communities share or contest collective memories and myths about 'ancestral homelands' that may never have been visited by some members of the community. The homeland may be seen as being a source of values, identities and loyalty as the 'true', ideal home (Cohen, 1991; Morley, 2001). These values and myths may find expression through community festivals and cultural events.

It is suggested that diasporic communities preserve distinctive identities based on dense and complex local and trans-national social and economic relationships (Christiansen, 1998). There is a question of the extent to which such boundaries are maintained over generations and how far they may be balanced and eroded over time by hybridity, fluidity and integration with indigenous communities. There is also a need to be wary of ascribing homogenised imaginary ethnic diasporic group coherence. In the case of 'the' Chinese, for example, there are strongly distinct affinities reflecting different language groups (Mandarin, Cantonese, Vietnamese and Hakka) and to the regions, villages and cities to which people trace their origins and ancestry (Benton and Pieke, 1998).

Ascription of peoples to a diasporic group is therefore problematic. There is a composite of racial (ethnic), cultural and social criteria involving varying degrees of assimilation, shared or conflicting experiences and memories, physical dispersal and inter-marriage. The boundaries and 'membership' of a diasporic community, the extent to which temporary migrants, for example from China, connect with diasporas who are permanent residents and with other local communities are examples of questions that are open to analysis in the context of festivals and cultural events (Cheung, 2004).

Art forms and cultural expressions associated with diasporic communities include literature, music, performance and visual arts as well as festivals and cultural events (Ong and Nonini, 1997). These may also express a complex, fluid and dynamic hybrid community identity, shaped by varying levels of artistic cross-fertilisation with indigenous cultures, offering a rich area for research.

Ethnic Chinese diasporas

There has been a long-standing culture of emigration from China to foreign lands with destinations often selected on the basis of extended family links to home villages and regions, so called 'chain migration' (Chan, 1983; Cheung, 2004; Poston and Mei-Yu, 1990). Manchester, for example was found in this research to include many people within its local Chinese community who traced their origins to the city region of Wuhan.

Emigration from China grew following the Communist assumption of power in 1949 and reached unprecedented levels following Chinese government reforms in 1978 and 1985 (Benton and Pieke, 1998). A growth in migration was also experienced from Hong Kong in the period up to the handover of power from the UK to China in 1997.

Chinese emigrants have played a major part as labour in the economies set up by Western colonialists and settlers in the Americas, Australia and Africa and in the merchant shipping, railway, construction and agricultural industries (Chan, 1983; Sinn, 1988). In Europe, Chinese people were recruited as contract labour in major port cities before the Second World War and were used, in part to break union power among European seamen. Connections with the English city of Liverpool, for example can be traced to this period (Benton and Pieke, 1998; Craggs and Loh-Lynn, 1985).

At least six major groups of Chinese migrants have spread across Europe, mainly over the past hundred years. These people originated from different regions of China, speaking mutually unintelligible languages or dialects and arriving more or less independently from each other. These migrants include:

1. People from southern Zhejiang recruited as contract workers.
2. Cantonese people from the Pearl River Delta and Hong Kong arriving at the major ports as seamen.
3. People of Chinese origin from Indochina after the fall of US backed regimes in Vietnam, Laos and Cambodia and subsequent war with China.
4. Chinese emigrants following decolonisation, including people from Indonesia moving to Holland and Chinese people from the former

British colonies such as Singapore and Malaysia from the 1960s–1970s.

5. People from northern Fujian province arriving in Europe from the 1980s and often associated with the activities of human traffickers ('snakeheads' or *Shetou*). There is a continuing problem with gang masters recruiting (and exploiting) contract labour for the agricultural and construction sectors in the UK. The Morecambe Bay tragedy in 2004, where more than 20 Chinese people drowned while cockle picking highlighted this continuing problem of exploitation, poor housing and the dangerous working conditions experienced by these migrants.

6. Migration to Eastern European countries following the fall of Communist regimes in the early 1990s. Many people in these communities are well educated city dwellers from Northern China (Benton and Pieke, 1998).

These variations in the origins of Chinese diasporic communities reinforce the point that such communities must not be assumed to be homogeneous. The complex histories of the Chinese overseas also suggest that British urban authorities and agencies need to have a clear appreciation of the backgrounds and inter and intra communal relations in 'their' local Chinese communities when engaging with them in connection with festival programmes.

The identities and cultural traditions of Chinese people overseas are commonly stereotyped as involving the pursuit of moral and cultural continuities with the homeland and values associated with Confucianism (Cohen, 1991). There is also seen to be an emphasis on links of obligation and patronage and the importance of 'preserving face' (maintaining family prestige and status) (Wang, 2000). Assumptions are also made that the Chinese see themselves as transient and therefore uncommitted to the places to which they have migrated. There is also seen to be an inherent emphasis on educational and artistic ideals and abstract visions of Han Chinese unity as core aspects of Chinese diaspora community identity (Cheung, 2004).

It is therefore typically suggested that overseas Chinese communities share distinctive assets such as moral and cultural institutions, images, roots, lifestyles, with festivals and cultural events expressing these. However, it is also recognised that there may, within a community, be disagreements over how to use, share and interpret these assets. It is thus all too easy to stereotype 'the' Chinese community. Chinese cultural assets are arenas for debate, competition and conflict as well as possible incorporation into wider city marketing, cultural, tourism, community development and regeneration discourses and programmes (Christiansen, 1998: 42).

The Chinese community in the UK

People of Chinese ethnicity are one of the largest, longest established and most widely dispersed diasporic communities in the UK, with 226,948 people or 0.4% of the UK population reported as being ethnically Chinese in the 2001 census (Chau and Yu, 2001). The Chinese diaspora community is widely dispersed across the UK, making up no more than 1% of the population of any UK city or region (Benton and Pieke, 1998). Chinese people are most conspicuous as an ethnic minority in Northern Ireland. Britain's Chinese community mainly comprises people who can trace their origins to Hong Kong, Singapore and Malaysia, with some more recent arrivals from Vietnam. This community profile is remarkably uniform, to the almost total exclusion of other Chinese groups (Benton and Pieke, 1998; Cheng, 1996; Jones, 1979; Ng, 1968; Owen, 1994).

Cantonese and Hakka are the main dialect groups of the British Chinese community. Mandarin and Vietnamese are also spoken, but to a much lesser extent. About a quarter of the community were born in Britain, with the rest coming from Singapore, Malaysia, Vietnam and mainland China. Most immigrants from Hong Kong came as 'economic migrants' between the late 1950s to late 1960s, resulting in a youthful to middle aged second generation of ethnic Chinese Britons. 50,000 Hong Kong families were given British citizenship at the handover of sovereignty to China in 1997. However, there is no data on the proportion of this group that has actually settled in the UK, with the likelihood being that it is fairly low as people either chose to remain in Hong Kong or to emigrate to Canada, the USA or Australia (Chau and Yu, 2001).

The Chinese diaspora community in the UK is characterised by high self-employment rates mainly associated with catering businesses, though many members of the second generation community are now entering other professions. There is a relatively high level of educational attainment (Benton, 2003).

The British Chinese are seen as being a 'quiet' community, experiencing limited racism as compared with some other 'ethnic' communities. However, the British Chinese seem also to have limited political and social significance, rarely attracting government attention. This is reflected in the very small number of ethnic Chinese people involved in British politics as elected members or in professional public sector occupations, for example (Cheng, 1996; Shang, 1984). They are seen as being heavily influenced by 'traditional' values and ways of life, centring on extended family and regional origin networks that constrain integration into 'mainstream' society. This portrayal may though be criticised as being stereotypical (Chau and Yu, 2001: 110).

It is unclear whether there is a distinctive British Chinese culture. Chinese festivals and community events in the UK for example appear to reflect traditional themes and formats with little adaptation to the UK national or local context. British Chinese artistic themes and cultural products are promoted by the British Chinese Arts Association, but these are arguably less conspicuous and commercially successful in comparison with the outputs of their British South Asian and Afro-Caribbean counterparts.

Overseas Chinese community organisations and associations

Chinese community associations and local organisations have been established in the UK since the early 1990s and are significant actors in the organisation of festivals in British cities.

These associations include those that draw their membership from students at British universities who are temporarily resident in the UK — the Chinese Students and Scholars Association (CSSA). There are 71 such associations in the UK, with several branches in the largest university cities. It is though suggested that these associations and their membership are typically "outside and above the British Chinatown milieu" (Christiansen, 1998: p. 45). This argument might usefully be examined in the context of the extent to which they interact and engage with resident British Chinese community associations in the organisation of festivals and cultural events.

British Chinese Community associations typically draw their membership on the basis of:

- Surname (e.g. Cheung, Man, Tang), reflecting a belief in shared ancestry;
- Shared provenance (e.g. those that emigrated from the same region);

- Shared language and/or dialect;
- Shared ideology and political principles, with the Union of Chinese Associations in Europe sponsored by Taiwan, and the European Federation of Chinese Organisations promoted by the People's Republic of China.

However, according to Benton and Pieke (1998: p. 12) these associations may often exist in name only and they may have little relevance in the wider community.

Chinese community associations have tended to be inward-looking and focused on providing social and educational benefits for community members, as well as links with the homeland. However, some have recently become more engaged with host societies and institutions, with the European Federation of Chinese Organisations (EFCO), for example adopting a lobbying role at the European Union. There are also more connections being forged with local government and other city institutions, with these links often associated with the organisation of festivals and cultural events. There is also a network of local Chinese community and social centres in UK cities that offer meeting places for elderly members of the first generation community, weekend and evening classes in language and culture, as well as social services and housing advice for Chinese communities.

Chinatown UK

'Chinatown' districts in cities internationally trace their origins to areas that emerged and were identified as such in San Francisco, London, Liverpool and New York for example, more than 100 years ago (Chan, 1983; Craggs and Loh Lynn, 1985; Lau, 2002). Chinatowns have typically developed as compact residential, production and service quarters for overseas Chinese populations and commonly formed as a result of low spatial mobility, experiences of racist hostility on the part of some in the indigenous community, subsequent ghettoisation, and an ability to dominate the property market in a small area.

Chinatowns may be seen as representing contested symbols of belonging and identity, functions, structures, ownership, competition and power within ethnic Chinese communities as well as more recent and developing relationships with wider local and city communities and institutions (Christiansen, 1998: 42).

Chinatowns in European cities are typically characterised by areas containing some (often a very few) streets comprising Chinese restaurants, groceries, supermarkets, betting establishments, pharmacies, acupuncture and herbal medicine clinics, travel agencies, bank branches, solicitors, bookshops and curio sellers. In some places, a very limited number of Chinese owned and/or themed businesses have been sufficient to justify a Chinatown label. However, it should be noted that members of ethnic Chinese British communities tend not to live in Chinatowns, most do not work in Chinatowns and few even shop there (Christiansen, 1998: p. 47).

'Chinatown' themed districts have emerged and developed in London, Manchester, Birmingham, Newcastle and Liverpool over the years, providing a focal point for Chinese culture, people and businesses and as attraction for city residents, tourists and shoppers seeking more or less 'authentic' Chinese products and foods (Lau, 2002). This concentration and place recognition can contribute to a competitive strategy for Chinese enterprises in being located in areas of critical mass that are recognised and that have developed a reputation over a period of years as being a site for 'authentic', differentiated and high quality restaurants and shops. However, and in contrast, the dispersed nature of the Chinese community in the UK reflects an alternative strategy for restaurant and take-away proprietors, where competition has been minimised or avoided through location in small towns and suburbs (Cheng, 1996).

Chinatowns in UK cities have been re-launched and packaged through joint efforts by local councils and overseas Chinese entrepreneurs from the 1980s as part of wider inner-city regeneration, area improvement, cultural and social programmes. Chinatown areas are increasingly marked out on maps and in city guides that are aimed at tourists and as a means of claiming an ethnically diverse inter-cultural city. The promotion of Chinatowns may also be linked with city institutions' wishes to attract Chinese business and student interest through the highlighting of a vibrant 'local Chinese' community.

This growing recognition and promotion has a symbolic cultural consequence in the growth of Chinese New Year celebrations as public spectacles that are multicultural in ethos and that are increasingly enjoyed by non-Chinese people (Christiansen, 1998: 49). Benton and Pieke (1998, 83) also suggest that this promotion of Chinatowns reflects new forms of urban political mobilization within Chinese communities in Britain. Chinatowns therefore, now function as sites and venues for major cultural, community events that attract non-Chinese city resident as well as tourist participation.

Chinese community festivals

Diasporic community festivals have not been much studied. Such festivals though are of considerable interest as sites where diasporic community traditions, relationships, and artistic idioms and practices are re-invented, interpreted and performed for audiences from within and beyond the community. Such events are also of increasing interest to city government policy makers and professional officers concerned with social inclusion, community development and participation as well as those officers responsible for city marketing, place promotion, tourism and developing an inter-cultural image of a city (Wood, 2005). Diaspora community festivals therefore relate to a wide range of policy domains.

The Chinese New Year (or Spring Festival) is the pre-eminent annual event in Chinese communities' cultural calendar and the most significant holiday period. The actual day of the New Year varies as the end of the 12 month lunar cycle flows between January and February. Essentially, the festival celebrates the end of winter, the earth coming back to life and the start of ploughing and sowing. During the 15-day period of celebrations the old year and its bad luck and problems is cast aside, old debts are cleared, the house is cleaned and if possible fresh flowers, in particular peach blossom is brought in. The New Year is seen as the luckiest time of the year to buy new goods.

Prior to the New Year Day red packets of lucky money will be collected and sweets stockpiled. On New Year's Eve fireworks are lit at midnight to drive away bad spirits. On New Year Day families visit friends and relatives, with gifts exchanged the following day. The celebrations continue through to day 15 when the lantern festival brings the proceedings to a close. It is important to note that much of this traditional pattern of celebration is private, family and community oriented, rather than being open to the public gaze and participation (Lau, 2002).

However, a prominent public dimension of the Spring Festival events is organised 'to allow everyone to participate, "with an intact face through displays of sharing and generosity. At large ceremonies, participants who are known to have opposing views or mutual grudges, or even to be involved in vendetta-like conflicts, demonstrate unity and amity" (Christiansen, 1998: p. 51).

The public festival typically includes lion and dragon dances, lantern parades, performances by Chinese folk and opera musicians, dance, acrobatics and martial arts. In British cities these events are held either in open air settings in Chinatowns or in entertainment, civic and / or university venues. Other main Chinese festivals that are celebrated in British cities include the Dragon Boat Festival at the start of the fifth lunar month (May-June) and the Mid-Autumn or Moon Festival which marks the time when the moon is furthest from the Earth and is said to be perfectly round. This is also a time when harvests are celebrated through feasting and the giving of gifts (Lau, 2002).

The celebration of Chinese festivals, and in particular the New Year Spring Festival appear to be increasingly prominent and 'officially' marked in British cities, including the involvement of local government tourism, arts and community development interests in partnership with British Chinese and visiting Chinese community associations and businesses. It may be that Chinese festivals are entering into the arena of competition between cities for business, student recruitment and tourism. The sections that follow explore these issues through brief case studies of Chinese festivals in three northern English cities.

Methodology: Recreating China in Manchester, Sheffield and York

This research aimed to explore the phenomenon of Chinese festivals and cultural events in three contrasting cities in the north of England. While the cities of Sheffield, Manchester and York were selected partly on the grounds of convenience, there were distinguishing features of the cities that made them interesting case studies for this research.

Manchester is a major post-industrial city with a relatively large British Chinese community that has been resident for many years. Manchester also has a designated Chinatown district in the heart of a regenerating and increasingly fashionable city centre. Sheffield is also a large multi-cultural city with a significant British Chinese community. There is an emerging though unofficial Chinatown district close to the city centre with recently opened and up market, 'Asian fusion' cuisine restaurants alongside other Chinese businesses and an established local Chinese community centre. York is a significant 'heritage tourism' city destination but with a relatively small ethnic minority resident community. Each city includes major universities and other higher education establishments that recruit significant numbers of Chinese students. Branches of the CSSA are also to be found in each city.

The researchers sought interviews with spokespeople for the British Chinese community in each city. Individuals were identified in Manchester and Sheffield through a Chinese business association in Manchester and the Chinese community centre in Sheffield. It was not possible to identify an individual representative of the Chinese community in York, reflecting its small population in that city. Interviews were sought with representatives of the CSSA in each city, and were also conducted with tourism, arts and culture officers of the councils in each of the three cities. Tourism and Cultural policy and strategy documents produced by City Councils and other relevant agencies were scrutinised by the researchers for explicit and implicit references to Chinese community festivals.

It should be noted that many ethnic Chinese British people speak Cantonese as their first language. Therefore, some issues of translation were apparent during the interviews where the first language of one of the interviewers is Mandarin. These languages are mutually recognisable in script form but are very different when spoken. The interviewers also noted that issues of protocol and the Chinese tradition of 'saving face' may have biased some responses. These methodological issues need to be given careful consideration in future research with Chinese interviewees.

Chinese community festivals in Manchester

Manchester's Chinatown is situated centrally in the city centre district known as Piccadilly. The first Chinese settlers arrived in Manchester in the early part of the 20th century. Proximity to Liverpool and a thriving industrial sector made Manchester the most natural city for the Chinese community to expand into. The Chinese came mainly as individuals, engaged in the laundry trade. Chinese people arrived in the city in greater numbers from the 1940s, but even then, numbered under one hundred. The first Chinese restaurant to open in Manchester did so in 1948 (the Ping Hong in Mosley Street). Over the next 12 years 16 more restaurants were to open. The boom continued well into the 1960s and 1970s. In 1962 the Willow Garden restaurant (now closed) opened with a capacity of 600 customers (Lau, 2002).

Chinatown 'status' was officially recognised when the Duke of Edinburgh unveiled the replica Ming Dynasty Imperial Arch that straddles Nicholas and Faulkner Streets. Britain's first Chinese Arts centre opened its doors in Charlotte Street in 1989 (now relocated) and for a while Manchester was seen as having one of Britain's most vibrant Chinese communities in Britain. However, Manchester's Chinatown failed to keep up with the pace of business expansion that happened in London during the 1990s (http://www.chinatown-online.co.uk/pages/guide/manchester/history.html). More recently though, the Chinatown district has revived along with regeneration programmes and the boom in Manchester's property market.

Spring festival celebrations have been organized in Manchester since the 1980s. These celebrations have been arranged by various organizations. One coordinating body is a 'function committee' representing several organizations that represent the locally resident Chinese community. Coordination is also provided by the CSSA of Manchester. The festival is sponsored by the Consulate General of the People's Republic of China in Manchester, and is supported by other, mainly British Chinese owned commercial organisations. In recent years and in 2005 the Spring Festival Evening Show holds its main staged event at the Bruntwood Theatre. The People's Republic of China Consul General based in Manchester, and the Lord Mayor of Manchester attended this event.

In an interview with the authors, a leading Chinese business man based in Manchester who had played a main role in organizing the New Year Festival in Chinatown for the past three years suggested that there had been some tensions over the arrangements. He suggested that there had been 'jealousy' expressed from within the community as there was a view that he had personally benefited from its recent success. He has since withdrawn from the festival committee as a result of this. However, in his view the festivals that have been held in the past three years have not satisfied the Chinese community, as they have not been as "splendid" as they used to be. In his account, the local Chinese community and representative organizations have donated funds for the festivals, but that these have not been properly used. These comments however, warrant further research with other stakeholders in the city's festival. It is likely that others from the Chinese community would hold contrasting views.

The City Council Arts Officer emphasised the growing popularity of Chinese festivities among the wider community and in particular the young professional classes who make up recent residents in city centre apartments. The important role played by a British Chinese Highways Officer at the Council in the management of the event and in liaison with the Chinese business community was also emphasised by this interviewee.

Chinese community festivals in Sheffield

The resident community of Chinese origin in Sheffield numbers approximately 5,000 people with an additional estimated 2,000 Chinese students at the city's two universities. Chinese people settled in the city from the 1950s with Hakka and Cantonese speakers from Hong Kong and the New Territories comprising the majority of the community. More recently, Mandarin speakers from other regions of China and Vietnam have come to the city, with the manager of the Chinese community centre estimating that speakers of Mandarin as a first language now make up around 30% of the community, with this proportion growing.

First generation immigrants largely developed restaurant businesses or worked for others in the Chinese catering industry. The second generation are now more involved in 'mainstream' occupations including law and business. However, and in common with the picture elsewhere, the ethnic Chinese community is seen as being under-represented in public sector professional occupations and as elected members in local politics (interview with Chinese Community Centre manager).

New ethnic Chinese arrivals in the city are coming to Britain under work permit schemes, including specialist chefs in regional Chinese cuisines. Chinese-British entrepreneurs are also recruiting skills from Hong Kong and China. These arrangements are however becoming more problematic as immigration and visa restrictions are tightened by the British government.

The Chinese takeaway and restaurant trade in Sheffield was originally dispersed around the suburbs, avoiding competition. However, there is now a clustering and 'critical mass' of diverse Chinese businesses emerging in the London Road and Sharrow district of the city — a highly multi-cultural area. Indeed there are moves to designate this area officially as a new 'Chinatown'. A Chinese supermarket opened here in the 1970s and the area has recently seen the opening of a number of both expensive and up-market as well as cheaper Chinese and Asian 'fusion' restaurants. Chinese herbalists and medical establishments, travel agencies and law practices aimed at the Chinese community have also opened in the area.

The New Year Festival has been organized formally in Sheffield by the local Chinese community, coordinated by the Sheffield Chinese Community Centre (SCCC) and the local universities branch of the CSSA only since 2004. The SCCC was set up in the Sharrow district of the city in 1995. It provides a range of services and activities by and for the Chinese population in Sheffield.

The centre runs two main projects. The first of these focuses on assisting the Chinese community in accessing mainstream health and social services. The second ongoing project involves encouraging community participation and volunteering work among Chinese youths. Other Chinese Community Centre activities include the provision of courses in English, Chinese Art and Dragon Dancing. There is also Chinese Song Society based at the Centre. The SCCC works with the City Council on community cohesion and regeneration programmes.

The SCCC has been instrumental in organising the New Year and other Chinese themed festivals in the city only very recently. As the Centre Manager put it, before 2004, Chinese community festivals had taken place 'behind closed doors'. The Centre has also contributed to the annual Sharrow Festival, a multicultural event reflecting the diverse population of the district. This work indicates how Chinese cultural expressions may be incorporated within wider inter-cultural festival programmes and cultural events.

In relation to the New Year festival, the community centre's role has involved coordinating the efforts of local Chinese associations and the branch of the CSSA. The Centre's premises provides a base for the production of decorated costumes, stages, masks, flags, banners, posters etc. involving the Chinese Women's Group, children and the Chinese Christian Association. The CSSA assisted with the design of the festival programme and the identification of performers. Sheffield City Council contributed to the promotion of the New Year celebrations through its Events Unit and through a small grant. Funding was also secured through ticket sales, fundraising among the Chinese community and a limited amount of commercial sponsorship.

The opening event at the 2005 New Year festival was held at the Octagon Centre of Sheffield University, and was organized by the

Sheffield Chinese New Year Celebration Committee. This is the collective name for the six individual Chinese groups in and around Sheffield. These are the Sheffield Chinese Community Centre; Sheffield CSSA; the University of Sheffield Chinese Society; Sheffield and District Chinese Association; Sheffield Chinese Christian Church and the Lai Yin Association. These six groups are responsible not only for organising the show but also in bringing together individuals, families, communities, and groups from Sheffield and beyond to participate in the event on Chinese New Year's Day. The number of groups involved highlights the complexity in Chinese festival organisation.

The People's Republic of China Consulate General, based in Manchester, and the Mayor of Sheffield attended the celebration. The programme involved students from CSSA Sheffield, children from the CSSA Star Mandarin School and invited actors from the Shenzhen Performing Artists of China. The regional channels of ITV and the BBC reported the event, and the Sheffield Star and Telegraph newspapers published reports and photographs of the performances.

Chinese community festivals in York

Data from the 2001 Census reveals that York's population is 97.8% white (compared with an average of 91.3% for England and Wales). However, of the Black and Minority Ethnic groups within York, the Census shows that people belonging to Chinese ethnic groups constitute the largest group within the city, comprising 642 people (a total of 0.35% of the total population of York). However, this represents a significant increase from the 1991 census return (Chau and Yu, 2001).

In spite of its small number, the ethnic Chinese community in York is long established. As Benton (2003: p. 351), reports, "York, a hundred miles from the nearest Chinatown, had a Siyinese run laundry as early as 1910 and eighteen Siyinese residents by 1921. In 1938, they and their relatives were running seven laundries in the city'. This trade has since largely disappeared, in common with cities elsewhere in the UK, and the community is now primarily engaged in the catering and restaurant trade.

The British ethnic Chinese community in York is therefore small and dispersed and there are no dedicated facilities or centre of community life (apart from ethnic Chinese Christians meeting at St. Michael le Belfry church). It is therefore difficult for cultural and social programme officers to make contact with 'representatives' of the community.

A local community development officer who has worked with the Chinese community in the city suggested that ethnic Chinese people tend to shop at Chinese supermarkets in Leeds and that they also send their children to schools in that city. However, the same interviewee also noted that 'York is becoming more Chinese' with around 900 students currently recruited from China by local higher education institutions, with this number set to grow. This interviewee also noted that the cultural diversity agenda is of growing importance in York with a particular emphasis on 'awareness raising' among the local community and improving race relations. The promotion of Chinese festivals was seen as being a good way of engaging with this agenda. Links were also being made with social inclusion and education programmes in the city.

In the context of the city's arts and cultural provision, the City Cultural Officer noted that the former York Arts Centre had closed several years ago and that there was a wish to retain and develop parts of its programming, notably 'world music'. Promoting Chinese arts and culture is strongly consistent with this cultural agenda.

Chinese arts in the city are currently promoted as part of 'world music' events at the National Centre for Early Music (NCEM), for example. The NCEM based in a former historic church and supported by Arts Council funding, views Chinese performances as fitting well with its artistic programme. Chinese artists are secured through the Chinese Arts Centre in Manchester and the Asian Music Circuit in London. 'World music' is seen as a good platform for audience development, including the specific targeting of ethnic Chinese residents who are under-represented in audiences for the arts in the city as well as other non-ethnic Chinese audiences and visiting Chinese people.

There is also considerable private sector interest in Chinese business markets, with HSBC Bank and Norwich Union both having sponsored Chinese themed cultural events and performances in York. Both companies are major employers in the city. As the City Council's Cultural Officer put it, obtaining business support for Chinese festivals, cultural events and performances is 'the easiest fundraising ever'. Chinese inward investment and business opportunities are also a priority for Yorkshire Forward, the regional development agency. York has been designated as a 'Science City' with specialisms in biosciences, IT and digital sectors and heritage conservation techniques. All of these are seen as being of interest to Chinese businesses and government.

There is also keen interest from the city tourism agency, First Stop York in the potential market for the city's tourism represented by the emerging and rapidly growing outbound Chinese tourist market (WTO, 2003). This interest is topical and understandable in view of the UK recently achieving 'approved destination' status from the Chinese government. Delegations of Chinese tourism business and heritage management professionals had recently visited the city and the Council is keen to develop and capitalise on these links as the city is seen as having expertise in these areas.

The presentation of the city as being open to Chinese culture and the arts is therefore unsurprising in this context. First Stop York also promotes York as a 'City of Festivals', with Chinese cultural events being very much a part of this 'brand'.

The celebration of the 2005 Spring Festival in York was held at the theatre of the Music Department of York University by the CSSA branch in the city. The attendees included the Vice Chancellor of York University, the deans from different university departments and the Vice President of CSSA UK. The programme involved singing, dancing, Chinese martial arts, storytelling, and musical performances. Artists were secured through the Chinese Arts Centre in Manchester. There are very few locally resident Chinese artists and performers in York.

Conclusions and recommendations for further research

The growing importance of China in the world cannot be denied. Indicators of economic growth, political and social change are the subject of widespread reporting and commentary from researchers, government agencies and the media alike. In common with cities and regions elsewhere in the UK, the private sector and public sector agencies in Manchester, Sheffield and York are keen to capitalise on potential business opportunities that may be developed with China. City tourism agencies are also keen to attract what they see as emerging and fast growing outbound Chinese tourist markets. Universities are competing to recruit Chinese students to their courses in the UK. British tourist destinations, businesses and universities are of course all facing global competition for Chinese trade, tourists and students.

Being seen to be culturally 'open for business' with China may be an important element in British cities competitive armoury. Long established links between local ethnic Chinese residents and 'homeland' Chinese cities and regions could be significant in this connection. It is likely that much business is already taking place between Chinese businesses in British cities and the 'homeland' beyond the view of city and regional chambers of commerce and regeneration agencies. However, there may be a risk that in their anxiety to develop formal, 'official' business relationships, local authorities and agencies may present stereotypical views of the tastes, interests and needs of Chinese tourists, students and business people.

The staging of Chinese community festivals in British cities seems to be a part of this 'cultural business diplomacy' but there are many questions that would warrant further research. This paper has presented some exploratory findings in the rich, interesting and complex area of diaspora community festivals. Further research might examine a number of issues in more detail. These include the inter-generational, occupational, residential, commercial and dynamic profile of the 'local' British Chinese community and the implications of these for the organisation of Chinese festivals in particular cities.

Evidence from the three case studies in this research suggests that the organisation of festivals may provide a platform for the development of relationships between and within the local Chinese community and with visiting Chinese business people and students. These relationships would also benefit from further research.

The relationships between British Chinese communities and local government tourism, arts, culture and community officers and agencies, and the ways in which British Chinese people may best present their interests and wishes to these agencies in connection with festivals also bears further examination.

Chinese festivals as staged in British cities would also warrant more research for example in relation to the extent to which their themes, programmes and performances reflect tradition and whether local adaptations and interpretations occur. The ways in which local non-ethnic Chinese communities participate in and experience Chinese festivals would also be of interest in the context of inter-cultural relations and the relative 'invisibility' of the Chinese community.

The ways in which city institutions, authorities and agencies get involved in Chinese festivals and the perceptions of these agencies in terms of the festival's roles in the arts, culture, community development, regeneration and tourism agendas would also be of interest. In connection with tourism, 'Chinese visitors may not just go to Paris or London, they may go to the Chinatowns, where the use of space, Chinese characters on facades, designs, smells, sights and sound of language may give reminiscence of an abstract Chinese world' (Christiansen, 1998: p. 48).

References

Axel, B. K. (2002) 'National interruption: Diaspora theory and multiculturalism in the UK', *Cultural Dynamics* (November) Vol. 14, No. 3 pp. 235–256.

Baker, H. (1994) 'Branches all over: The Hong Kong Chinese in the United Kingdon', in Skeldon, R. (ed) *Reluctant exiles? Migration from Hong Kong and the new overseas Chinese.* Armonk, NY: M.E. Sharpe, pp. 291–307.

Barone, G. (1991) 'Travelling heavy – the intellectual baggage of the Chinese diaspora', *Problems of communism* Vol. 40, No. 1–2: pp. 94–112.

Baxter, S. and Raw, G. (1988), 'Fast food, fettered work: Chinese women in the ethnic catering industry', in S. Westwood and P. Bhachu (eds) *Enterprising women.*

Benton, G. (2003) 'Chinese transnationalism in Britain: A longer history', *Identities: Global Studies in Culture and Power,* 10: pp. 347–375.

Benton, G. and Pieke, F. (eds) (1998) *The Chinese in Europe.* Basingstoke: Macmillan.

Benton, G. and Vermeulen, H. (1987) *The Chinese: Migrants in Dutch society.* Muidenbergh: Coutinho.

Brubaker, R. (2005) 'The 'diaspora' diaspora', *Ethnic and racial studies* (January) Vol. 28, No. 1: pp. 1–19.

Campbell, P. C. (1923). *Chinese coolie emigration to countries within the British Empire.* London: P. S. King and Son.

Chan, A. (1986) *Employment prospects of Chinese youth in Britain: A research report.* London: Commission for Racial Inequality.

Chan, A. B. (1983) *Gold mountain: The Chinese in the New World.* Vancouver: New Star Books.

Chau, R. and Yu, S. (2001) 'Social exclusion of Chinese people in Britain', *Critical Social Policy* Vol. 21, No. 1: pp. 103–125.

Cheng, Y. (1996) 'The Chinese. Upwardly mobile', in Ceri Peach (ed), *The ethnic minority populations of Great Britain, ethnicity in the 1991 Census*, Series 2. London: HMSO.

Cheung, G. (2004) Chinese aiaspora as a virtual nation: Interactive roles between economic and social capital, *Political Studies* 52: pp. 664–684.

Christiansen, F. (1998) 'Chinese Identity in Europe', in Benton, G. and Pieke, F. *(eds) The Chinese in Europe*. Basingstoke: Macmillan.

Cohen, M. L. (1991) 'Being Chinese: The peripheralization of traditional identity', *Daedalus* Vol. 20, No. 2: pp. 113–35.

Coles, T. and Timothy, D. J. (2004) *Tourism, diasporas and space*. London: Routledge.

Craggs, S. & Loh Lynn I. (1985) *A history of Liverpool's Chinese community*. Liverpool: Merseyside Community Relations.

Findlay, A.M. *et al.* (1995) 'The British who are not British and the immigration policies that are not: the case of Hong Kong', *Applied Geography* 15: pp. 245–65.

Findlay, A.M. and Li, F.L. (1997) 'An auto-biographical approach to understanding migration: The case of Hong Kong emigrants', *Area* 29: pp. 34–44.

Gungwu, W. (1991) 'Among non-Chinese', *Daedalus* Vol. 20, No. 2: pp. 135–158.

Guo, W., Turner, L. and King, B. (2002) 'The emerging age of Chinese tourism and its historical antecedents: A thematic investigation', *Tourism, Culture and Communication* Vol. 3 pp. 131–146.

Jones, D. (1979) 'The Chinese in Britain: Origins and development of a community', *New Community* Vol. 7, No. 3: pp. 397–402.

Lau, S. (2002) *Chinatown Britain*, London: Chinatown Online.

Lever-Tracy, C., Ip, D.F.K., and Tracy, N. (1996) *The Chinese diaspora and mainland China: an emerging economic synergy*. Basingstoke: St Martin's Press.

Lew, A. and Wong, A. (2004) 'Sojourners, *guanxi* and clan associations', in Coles, T. and Timothy, D. J. *Tourism, diasporas and space*. London: Routledge.

Lew, A. and Yu, L. (1995) *Tourism in China: Geographic, political and economic perspectives*. Boulder: Westview Press.

Li, F. and Findlay, A. (1996) 'Placing identity: Interviews with Hong Kong Chinese immigrants in Britain and Canada', *International Journal of Population Geography* 2: pp. 361–77.

Morley, D. (2001) 'Belongings: Place, space and identity in a mediated world', *European Journal of Cultural Studies* Vol. 4, No. 4: pp. 425–448.

Ng, K. C. (1968) *The Chinese in London*. London: Oxford University Press for the Institute of Race Relations.

Nurse, K. (2004) 'Festival tourism in the Caribbean: An economic impact assessment', in Long, P. and Robinson, M. (eds) *Festivals and tourism: Marketing, management and evaluation*. Sunderland: Business Education Publishers.

Nurse, K. (1999) The globalisation of Trinidad Carnival: Diaspora, hybridity and identity in global culture. *Cultural Studies* Vol. 13, No. 4: pp. 661–690.

Nyiri, P. (2001) 'Expatriating is patriotic? The discourse on "new migrants" in the People's Republic of China and identity construction among recent migrants from the PRC', *Journal of Ethnic and Migration Studies* Vol. 27, No. 4: pp. 635–653.

Ong, A and Nonini, D. (1997) *Ungrounded empires: The cultural politics of modern Chinese transnationalism*. London: Routledge.

Owen, D. (1994) *Chinese people and 'other' ethnic minorities in Great Britain: Social and economic circumstances*, 1991 Census Statistical Paper 8. University of Warwick, Centre for Research in Ethnic Relations.

Oxfeld, E. (1993) *Blood, sweat and majong: Family and enterprise in an overseas Chinese community*. Cornell University Press.

Parker, D. (1995) *Through different eyes: The cultural identities of young Chinese people in Britain*. Aldershot: Avebury.

Parker, D.J. (1994) 'Encounters across the counter: Young Chinese people in Britain', *New Community* Vol. 20, No. 4: pp. 621–34.

Poston, D. and Mei-Yu, Y. (1990) 'The distribution of overseas Chinese in the contemporary world', *International Migration Review*, 24: 480–508.

Shang, A. (1984) *The Chinese in Britain*. London: Batsford Academic and Educational.

Sinn, E. (ed) (1998) *The last half-century of Chinese overseas*. Hong Kong University Press.

Summerskill, M. (1982) *China on the western front: Britain's Chinese work force in the First World War*. London: Michael Summerskill.

Thompson, R. H. (1980) 'From kinship to class: A new model of urban overseas Chinese social organization', *Urban Anthropology* Vol. 9, No. 3: pp. 265–93.

Tu, W.M. (ed) (1994) *The living tree: The changing meaning of being Chinese today.*

Wah Y-Y, Avari, B. and Buckley, S. (1996) *British soil, Chinese roots.* Liverpool: Countyvise.

Wang, G. (2000) *The Chinese overseas: From earthbound China to the quest for autonomy.* Cambridge: Harvard University Press.

Werbner, P. (2004) 'Theorising complex diasporas: Purity and hybridity in the South Asian public sphere in Britain', *Journal of Ethnic and Migration Studies* (September) Vol. 30, No. 5: pp. 895–911.

Wood, P. (ed) (2005) *The intercultural city reader.* London: Comedia.

WTO (2003) *Chinese outbound tourism.* Madrid: World Tourism Organization.

UNICYCLING AT LAND'S END: CASE STUDY OF THE LAFROWDA FESTIVAL OF ST. JUST, CORNWALL

Rebecca Finkel

London Metropolitan University

Introduction

Festivals have traditionally been vehicles for expressing the relationship between identity and place (Turner, 1982: p. 11). Throughout European history from the 12th century onwards, public festivals have played an important role in raising civic consciousness (Muir, 1997) and facilitating the sense of collective belonging to a place (Ekman, 1999). It is the nature of festivals to bring people together for the celebration of shared histories and values, thereby propagating local continuity and forming and reforming local identities through ritually repeated actions (Quinn, 2005: p. 928).

The contemporary arts festivals that can be seen to best illustrate this connection between place, people and identity are those that depend mostly on personal donations from local residents and members of the community. By the act of giving to support these events, thereby making them happen, people are demonstrating their pride of place and desires to share in a collective experience with the rest of their community. Arts festivals that survive on primarily personal donations, as opposed to business sponsorship or government grants, usually are not big and very often take place in rural or non-urban areas. Because they are only responsible to their communities, their priorities do not tend to include tourism or place-based image-related goals. This lack of economic development agendas is one of the reasons they are often dismissed as insignificant in the contemporary cultural environment, as the recent trend among arts organisations and government funding bodies is to mainly view the arts as another 'cog' in the economy instead of being an important part of and belonging to the community (Lehrer, 2004).

129

However, it is these festivals that are in keeping with the traditional ideas of festivity that often provide tremendous social benefits to people and society. Links between arts festivals and communities have a long history, but they are not intrinsic in the nature of festivals. They must be cultivated and nurtured to achieve such outcomes (Quinn, 2005: p. 935). As Dayton-Johnson and King put it, "A festival is not like a factory or a mine, the outputs of which can be valued to the fraction of a cent each day. Many of the benefits of a festival are intangible in a way that steel or iron ore is not" (2003: p. 2). The narrow view that the purpose of arts festivals must be development or marketing-related is a rather new phenomenon and is indeed very limiting given the valuable potential arts festivals have for restoring civic engagement and participation (Quinn, 2005: p. 935; 937).

This paper focuses on one such community arts festival that relies on donations from local residents in order to continue from year to year, the Lafrowda Festival of St. Just in Cornwall. At first, there will be a review of the methodology undertaken for this case study and then a brief background of St. Just and the Lafrowda Festival, which will provide context in analysing the festival's aims and impacts. A discussion of the St. Just community and identity and the effects the festival youth development programmes have on the town will follow. It will conclude with an examination of broader contemporary festival funding and competition issues and what this could mean for the future of Lafrowda and similar small arts festivals that do not fit in to UK government cultural funding strategies or business sponsorship agendas.

Methodology

This case study is part of a PhD dissertation into the social, economic and political impacts of UK arts festivals on communities and places. Methodology for this research includes a survey sent to 117 arts festivals in the UK, with data based on a 56% response rate. Participant and direct observation at the 2004 Lafrowda Festival was undertaken, and in-depth interviews were conducted with Lafrowda Festival organisers and volunteers, St. Just youth workers and residents, the Penwith District Council arts officer and local press.

Shifts in policy and perceptions for the arts

In recent times, the UK government has encumbered cultural policy with a heavy responsibility that often extends far beyond the cultural realm. The arts in the UK have recently become increasingly entwined with political agendas and strategies that have little to do with aesthetics (Brighton, 2006: p. 116). Contemporary cultural policies can be understood to be no longer merely concerned with arts provision and arts appreciation, but are expected to "transform society" (Mirza, 2006: p.19). The increasing overlap of development and cultural policies can be seen to have roots in the current government agendas for the culture-led transformation of regions (Gibson and Klocker, 2005: p. 94). It is argued that public sector support for the arts is now more concerned with socio-economic outcomes as a result of arts provision, as opposed to simply the arts themselves (Belfiore, 2006: p. 21). It is argued that the government now interprets the arts in terms of commercial benefits and social priorities (Gibson and Klocker, 2005: p. 95), and, as a result, the UK cultural sector is becoming more target, rather than process oriented (Belfiore, 2006: p. 24). For example, the government has been putting pressure on arts organisations to help achieve targets for health, social inclusion, crime, education and community cohesion (Mirza, 2006: p. 14).

These uses of cultural forms as instruments for socio-economic developments are tied to the increasing competition among places for capital, residents, tourists, and so forth (Gibson and Klocker, 2005: p. 94). Place marketing through improving image, economic development and regeneration are often tied to cultural policies. The arts are considered dominant factors in regional 'success' and are often introduced as a panacea for places that are seeking economic development (Gibson and Klocker, 2005: p. 93). These socio-economic targets set out by the government have led arts organisations to spend much of their time measuring their impacts in different policy areas to prove they are worthy of their subsidy (Mirza, 2006: p. 14). Although, as Belfiore points out, there are no longer 'subsidies' according to the central government, but 'investments'. This can be interpreted as not merely a change in language, but a shift in expectations and perceptions (2006: p. 24).

The reason for this shift can be connected to New Labour's policy of "joined up government" (DCMS, 1998) or unifying control at the top level and disseminating policy to the levels below. Contemporary cultural planning initiatives in the UK were "strategically reclaimed" by the top levels of central government and are directed by the Department for Culture, Media and Sport (DCMS) (Selwood, 2006: p. 39). However, it is the responsibility of local governments to implement and respond to the community's specific cultural needs (Gibson and Klocker, 2005: p. 96). Each council in the UK was 'encouraged' to develop their own cultural strategy that conformed to the guidelines and targets set out by the DCMS (Selwood, 2006: p. 40). This can be seen as a move on the part of local councils beyond "traditional roles of physical and community infrastructure provision and finance" to become "modern facilitators of sustainable regional economic development" (National Economics, 2004: p. 1.7).

These shifts in policy and perceptions can be seen as one of the reasons that the role of arts festivals has shifted from the more traditional responsibilities of fostering community cohesion and ritualising local celebration to an emphasis on the 'collateral benefits of supporting the arts', which are usually economic in nature (Riding, 2005: p. E9). These economic dimensions seem to provide justification for public spending on the arts, as if an incredible artistic experience or widening education and exposure to the arts was not enough in its own right (Myerscough and Bruce, 1988: p. 2). As a result of these new cultural funding policies, it is the arts festivals who do not receive public support that are most in keeping with the traditional ideas of festivity and often provide tremendous social benefits to people and society. The narrow view that the purpose of arts festivals must be development or marketing-related is a rather new phenomenon and is indeed very limiting given the valuable potential arts festivals have for restoring civic engagement and participation (Quinn, 2005: p. 935; 937).

However, there recently has been an increase in attention from academic researchers in the field concerning the social benefits of festivals, especially those at a local community level. Although a range of social impact assessment and evaluation methodology has been developed (see Finsterbusch *et al.*, 1983; Wildman and Baker, 1985; Burdge, 1999; Barrow, 2000; Fredline *et al*, 2004; Sherwood *et al.*, 2005), there is still much work to be done in implementing a standard to be used consistently throughout the UK. Many of these studies are Australian, but would apply to a UK context if used in a similar manner. There also has been some research conducted concerning local festivals in the UK, which examine their social impacts on communities and places (see Rolfe, 1992; Smith, 1993; Small *et al.*, 2005). However, there is a need for further examination into the role of community arts festivals in the UK, as it is suggested that the impacts of the changes in government cultural policy and public perceptions on the local festival landscape has not been examined sufficiently. The following case study analyses what is happening to arts festivals at a local level in the context of wider social, political and economic concerns.

Expressions of Cornish pride: Case Study of the Lafrowda Festival

St. Just is the most westerly town in England with a population of around 4, 000 people. Its industrial history is in tin mining. Many of the mines have been closed in the past decade, and the village has felt the negative economic effects from these closures. St. Just is a working class town, and unlike nearby St. Ives, it is usually bypassed by retirees and tourists. There are some local artists who have moved in to the area, however, and they are instrumental in spearheading the Lafrowda Festival, which has been entertaining the locals of St. Just for a week before the school summer holidays for the past nine years.

Lafrowda is the old Cornish name for St. Just and was purposefully selected by the organisers to give the festival a link to local traditions and identity. The festival exists solely because of the dedication and hard work of over 40 volunteers. There is no money to pay employees and barely enough funding to scrape by each year. The festival relies primarily on personal donations and local business contributions, as the council does not financially support the festival. The council does provide basic logistical support in terms of public toilets being kept open and road closures. But on the whole, the town of St. Just puts on this festival by themselves and for themselves.

Example A is an excerpt from a research diary of personal experiences and observations of the 2004 Lafrowda Festival. It describes initial impressions of St. Just and local residents as they prepare for the Lafrowda Day activities.

Example A. Research Diary (July, Friday day):

St. Just is comprised of two main streets with five pubs that have huge hanging pots of flowers outside their doors. Barbara Smith, a festival volunteer and public relations manager, tells me the flowers have nothing to do with the festival, but are for the regional 'Blooms for Britain' competition. Posters for the Lafrowda Festival are hung in every window in the main square, from the pubs to the cafÈ to the chippie. As we walk past the school, two teenage boys on unicycles wobble towards us. They are involved in the circus training workshops and tell us proudly that they are leading the main parade on Lafrowda Day. The workshop leader provided one of the boys with a unicycle, but the other boy tells us that his neighbour had an old unicycle in his barn. I find this surprising, but Barbara assures me that there are some real characters in this part of the world. The boys cycle off to practise riding up and down hills, and Barbara comments that most people think it's great that the boys are on unicycles for the festival, but their perceptions of the boys would be completely different if they were on skateboards. There appears to be some tensions between young and old in this town, which I think the festival purposefully tries to address and assuage.The Nancherrow Youth Centre is a hub of activity with school kids putting finishing touches on their floats and banners. One girl is trying her papier-mache Venetian gondola on for size. Local artist Graham Jobbins is assembling some of the images that will lead the parade in Lafrowda Day. Graham is an artist of some renown, as he created the main sculpture for the Burning Man Festival in Nevada. At the moment, he has his head unceremoniously up the skirts of a topless ten-foot papier-mache Polynesian woman attempting to attach her hips in such a way to make them swing when she is carried in the parade. I am told that some of these parade 'images' are leftover from past festivals, but many are newly created by local school children depending on the overall parade theme. Last year's theme was 'the beach', whereas this year's is 'island paradise'. The images are kept from year-to-year in an old abandoned tin mine near Graham's house and in other people's barns, as there is no storage space in the youth centre or school.

Analysis of the content of the Lafrowda Festival

The first event of the festival each year is a steel drum band playing in the village square. Dot and Dave Stevens, festival organisers, say the steel band was chosen because it is loud and acts as a reminder to the town that this is festival week. Most concerts and performances take place outdoors (rain or shine) in the main square, streets and park. Some available community spaces, such as the school auditorium, are also used. The festival programme includes all types of music, folk dance, a carnival, street performances, parades, stilt walkers, fire shows, drama, musicals, storytelling and children's events. Events are free unless a local group charges admission for an event it is staging as part of the festival. For example, the St. Just Violin Group and the St. Just Operatic Society charge for performances to support their groups. On the whole, the festival does not generate revenue from performances. Volunteers with collection cans attend most events and ask for donations to support festival costs.

Example B sets out excerpts of personal observations from a research diary of attendance of outdoor evening activities at the 2004 Lafrowda Festival.

Example B. Research Diary (July, Friday evening):

We join the residents of the town in the main square to hear local bands perform on a small make-shift stage. Some resident audio technicians have volunteered their time and gear to set up a suitable sound system for the bands. Most people in the audience know the people on stage and are there to cheer them on. After the end of the set, the band yells "Lafrowda!" and the crowd echoes this. All the pubs are packed with people inside and outside on the picnic tables. Volunteers with collection tins make their rounds and almost every-one who is asked puts in coins. A woman [who] I am told is a salsa dancing instructor in town sports kool-aid red hair and gold shim-mery eye shadow and gives impromptu lessons to the teenage girls in flip flops and flimsy tops. Most of the crowd is white — I only see one black couple and one Chinese couple. There are lots of people in tie-dyed black and white clothes since these are the Cornish colours. Some of the men have their own pewter tankards, which are kept on a shelf in their favourite pub. Children and babies are welcome and dance along with the adults. This is truly a friendly, family festival. I feel my urban cynicism peeling away.

The Lafrowda Festival is almost wholly local with some visitors from neighbouring villages. Most of those coming from outside the town travel to St. Just for the parades on 'Lafrowda Day', which is the last Saturday of the festival. This small, localised audience makes programming the festival from year-to-year a challenge in that it is practically the same audience each year. Thus, the organisers try to vary content as much as possible. The main goal is to provide a variety of acts that appeal to different age ranges, while supporting local groups. As organiser Dot Stevens put it, "We may have a film and an opera on the same night since the film may appeal to younger people and the opera to older people." However, there are some 'staples' of the festival that the residents of St. Just look forward to attending each year. These are the children's parade, arts procession, battle of the bands, fire show and lantern procession that take place on Lafrowda Day. These events involve the local community and young people from the schools and youth centres in the area.

Example C is an account of personal experience in attending many of the 2004 Lafrowda Day events. This research diary entry illustrates the community cohesion element of the festival due to the involvement of almost all of the local population and school children from St. Just and the surrounding area.

Example C. Research Diary (July, Saturday day, Lafrowda Day!):

The next morning we are greeted by a torrential downpour. This is obviously not optimal festival weather. Yesterday, co-director Dot Stevens said she was hoping there wasn't going to be too much sun because people drink too much outside and get sun stroke and don't last the whole day. But she said it's also bad if it's too rainy because people spend the day in pub and not in streets, and it loses the festival feeling if people aren't in the streets. I don't particularly feel like being in the streets either, but I know how much work has gone into this festival and drag myself into town to watch a very cute, albeit very wet, children's parade. The rain eases up a bit as the little school children of St. Just parade through town in costumes covered in slickers and umbrellas shielding dripping face paint. By the time the music starts in the market square at noon, the sun is shining and the rain is a faint memory. Stalls selling anything from baked goods to sarongs are set up lining the streets of the village. Some people are selling their own crafts, while others are raising money for local groups or charities. The butchers and delicatessen have set up a big barbecue in front of one of the pubs. The smoke enshrouds half of the square, but nobody seems to mind as they queue for £3 bangers and burgers. In the cafÈ, there is hardly enough room for the guitar player with people elbowing through to order the Lafrowda Day hummus sandwich special. A terrible mariachi band serenades the crowds. The park, which is about 200 yards from the main square, has a second stage set up and a DJ is setting the laid- back scene with reggae music. Every inch of grass is filled with sunbathers and people of all ages listening to the music and drinking beer from plastic cups. Little kids run around in tiger costumes and pink sparkly tutus. A samba band begins to play as the young people set up their floats for the main procession. A reporter from *The Cornishman* newspaper is interviewing volunteers and is very impressed by how much has been done on a shoe-string budget. As outsiders, we are both amazed that the organisers actually do this and hold down full-time jobs and take care of children. Our conversation is interrupted by the unicyclists charging ahead with giant images of a sea monster and tree frog following behind. Each school and youth club has someone holding a sign announcing who they are in front of kids holding brightly-decorated banners and papier-mache suns and Mexican sombreros. The giant Polynesian lady we saw Graham assembling yesterday is clearly the favourite of the procession. Her head bobs and her hips swing as the four people holding her try to keep her from toppling into the crowds. There are a few thousand people lined up watching the procession, which is what I had expected from talking to the organisers, Dave and Dot Stevens. Dave said he estimates 5, 000 people attend Lafrowda Day (but less for each festival event during the week). He arrived at this number by counting cars in the village and multiplying that by three. He estimates that amounts to 2/3 of the people who live in the village, but thinks it could probably be more.

Youth focus

The festival organisers make it a point to engage young people with the festival. One way they do this is by getting the schools in the area involved in the festival activities. The festival supports arts education workshops throughout the year. Often this takes the form of a local artist coming in to schools and working with children. Also, there a number of after-school activities that the local youth centre co-ordinates in relation to the festival. For example, in the months leading up to the festival, the youth centre provides the space for volunteers to help kids to create the big images for the Lafrowda Day processions through town. Each year there is an overall theme, e.g., island paradise, and school children work with local artists to design and build parade floats. Younger children make Japanese lanterns for the lantern procession that closes the festival each year. There are not any cultural institutions or many cultural events in St. Just and its environs, which is why the festival is a non-threatening way to introduce young people to the arts. The festival also involves the participation of parents, thereby making it a family affair and helping to bring people together.

One of the more innovative activities the festival helps support is the training of teenagers in the art of circus skills. A local performer gives workshops to mainly disaffected youth in stilt walking, unicycling and fire juggling. The teens get to use their circus skills throughout the festival, and there is a fire show as one of the festival events with both the professionals and amateurs performing in the village square. Barbara Smith, festival volunteer, said, "The idea is these kids are probably going to set fires anyway, so they might as well do it to entertain." Local teenagers also get a chance to partake in a 'battle of the bands' during the festival. Jo Eccleston, co-ordinator of school workshops, said that the teens look forward to the event and take it very seriously. Thus, the festival gives them a public space and a chance to play in front of an audience.

A first-person account of the youth element of the festival is set out in Example D.

Example D. Research Diary (July, Saturday evening):

Later in the evening, the fire performance begins in the main square. The local young people give a demonstration first. They are dressed in black and come out swirling chains that are lit at the ends. They swirl the fire around their bodies, and a little girl does it really fast and without trepidation so that the crowd bursts into applause. Someone, I assume her mother, says loudly, "As long as she doesn't do it near the barn!" And the crowd erupts in laughter. The fire jugglers are not as adept and often drop a flaming ball into the crowd. Everyone backs up and continues to enjoy the spectacle. Once the last of the fires has been extinguished, the crowds line up on the street again for the last procession of the festival. Young children parade with Japanese lanterns that they have made. I can't see a thing since the crowds are three people deep. Most of the kids and families have gone by now, but the 'Hellblazers', who are the professional fire throwers, put on an extra-long show because the headline band for the evening is late coming back from Penzance. There is more heckling from the crowd for the late night shows, as the audiences are drunker. The square thins out around midnight, and then the volunteers must clean up everything that night. Mary Ann, co-founder of the festival, was complaining yesterday that many people in St. Just take the festival for granted, not realising the incredible amount of work goes into it. With this in mind, I pitch in and help clean up the square.

Mary Ann Bloomfield, a youth social worker and co-founder of the Lafrowda Festival, says she wanted to help change the negative image of young people by getting them involved in something positive in the village. Also, she wanted young people to take pride in where they live and feel they had ownership of something in the community. As she said, "When the tin mines closed, it was pretty grim around here. There was low morale, and people made poor jokes about St. Just. It really got to me. This is a unique community, and I wanted young people especially to recognise that and be a part of that." The festival aims to give young people an opportunity to showcase their creativity and feel a sense of pride in their home town.

Financial state

The entire Lafrowda Festival costs £12, 000. As stated above, the council provides very little financial help, and the festival relies on donations and local support. Organiser Dave Stevens says that people in the village "want the festival to happen, so they give £10 or £400. Whatever they can." This financial reliance on the festival audience literally gives ownership of the festival to the local people. As Stevens put it, '"Our audience is not a transient population like in a city. We can't alienate people because they'll come and tell us." This also has an interesting impact on festival growth in the future. While many small local festivals like Lafrowda are trying to grow and gain more recognition these days, this festival cannot afford wide-spread marketing and do not particularly want to become bigger and develop new audiences. It is understood that the money raised from local people and businesses will be spent on entertainment and education for the community and not spent trying to bring in more people to crowd the village. As organiser Dot Stevens said, "We can't get any bigger. The town is full." Any press the festival receives is aimed to show off the excellence of the festival and the hard work of its volunteers instead of trying to attract tourists to the events.

Sustainability matters

Instead of growth, the main concern is sustainability. Each year it is 'touch-and-go' as to whether the festival will be able to go forward. Cost of events is consistently an issue, and fundraising success will determine the number and type of events for the year. Organisers Dave and Dot Stevens said that outside funding was "big" in 2000 but not any longer. Kate Laird, Arts Council England Combined Arts Officer, feels this upsurge in grant giving around the millennium was a big mistake on the part of the government because funds are no longer available to sustain that initial period of financial support since the Millennium Grants ended in 2002. She said, "It raises expectations that then can't be met. We're faced with a situation now where we don't have a great big arts budget. So much has happened around the year 2000, and there's such a big whole afterwards." The Arts Councils and regional development agencies (RDA) can no longer afford to give money to festivals each year; therefore, any festival applying for a grant must be able to prove that it can sustain itself without Arts Council or RDA support. Giving one-off large grants is no longer part of the strategy to support the arts, as it "creates a false economy" (Laird, 2003).

The Lafrowda Festival is having trouble getting regional arts council grants because it is not seen as sustainable, and arts organisations and the district council are not willing to take the chance in giving it funding just in case it folds next year. Rose Barnecut, Arts, Culture & Media Officer of the Penwith District Council, confirmed that arts funding bodies now want to see readily measurable financial benefits over a period of time. She said the council wants festivals to no longer rely on council support and to create a firmer base independent from grant reliance. Regional and local councils now regard the promotion of regional tourism as their primary budget focus. In response to this, Colin McClary, Chair of Lafrowda Trust, says, "People want it [the festival], so we're going to do it. The council should get with the programme and help support it. Forget sustainability rubbish — it doesn't apply here. This is a community event. It's an honest festival."

This is not to say the council supports a 'dishonest' festival, but rather a different kind of festival — one that is larger, more visible and more in keeping with their sustainable entertainment goals. This is the Galowan Festival in Penzance. This festival attracts wider audiences from the region and visitors who have come to Cornwall for the summer. It runs for ten days and features professional artists and performers. Festival volunteers in St. Just do not see Galowan as competition because it is a "separate entity" and not considered a local arts festival. Ticket prices to some Galowan performances are seen as prohibitive for many people in St. Just, and the programming is said to have been "hijacked by art snobs" (Stevens, 2004). Because Galowan is not a community-owned event, the Lafrowda Festival volunteers feel it excludes many local people and have little time for it.

However, this kind of large, image-promoting, destination-making arts festival is becoming more of the norm than the smaller, more community-focused festivals like Lafrowda because they tend to receive more funding and support. Although festivals like Galowan tend to "tick more boxes" than those like Lafrowda, it would be a shame if there were no longer room for the Lafrowdas in the contemporary arts festival landscape. After all, the Edinbugh festival was not established with tourism objectives (Quinn, 2005: p. 933). But as more contenders vie for a decreasing pool of resources and interest is diverted to bigger spectacles in nearby cities, this could lead to a loss of place-based individuality for arts festivals and a loss of cultural diversity and local pride for communities.

Conclusions

With the increasing expectations that arts events should be a part of an industry that is professionally managed in order to achieve strategic goals, perhaps policy makers need to go back to widen their conceptions of what arts festivals are supposed to be about. There seems to be a contemporary focus on viewing arts events in narrow terms that relate to the economic. This is very limiting, considering the great potential and past achievement record they have for improvements to social benefits and development (Quinn, 2005: p. 935). It is argued that the perception of the arts as an economic instrument will eventually be detrimental to both the arts and society. The arts should matter to society for their own sake and not only as a means to an economic end (Bailey *et al.*, 2004: p. 64). Treating the arts as simply another area of public policy, administration and management (Gray, 2000: p. 4) may be taking the creativity, and therefore the very essence, out of what makes the arts so potent. As Hewison put it, "The arts are a means of empowering people to shape their own identities and destinies. But it won't be able to do that if they are seen as mere commodities, elite specialisms, niche marketing and other objects of economic exploitation" (in Robinson *et al.*, 1994: p. 32).

As the Lafrowda Festival demonstrates, arts festivals can make a very large social contribution to an area, and that fact seems to be getting buried these days. Improving social values and engaging communities in collective endeavour may not have demonstrable bottom-line or 'quick fix' solutions to societal woes in the here-and-now, but it returns on the investment in the future by helping to make better citizens, by strengthening communities, by enhancing overall quality of life and by making areas more attractive places to live (Myerscough and Bruce, 1988: p. 77). The focus should be, as Hewison put it, "Money for values not value for money" (in Robinson *et al.*, 1994: p. 32). It is imperative for government agencies to adopt a more holistic approach to validating their funding decisions and evaluating the impacts that the arts and arts events have on places. Without including social and even environmental valuations into impact assessments, the cycle of underestimating and undervaluing, and therefore underfunding, arts activities will continue to the possible detriment of communities and places (Sherwood *et al.*, 2005: p. 12).

As a thoroughly community sponsored and managed event, the Lafrowda Festival aims to create a sense of identity and pride in the people of St. Just. And the content of the festival reflects this goal. The festival widens access to and involvement in the arts in an area where cultural life is not vibrant. As an example of grassroots organisation and participation, it provides a platform for local performers and young people. The festival is driven more by a 'feel good factor' than a desire for name recognition or economic success. And council officials and arts organisations should be lauding it and not penalising it for that. This concept of recognising and supporting the social values of arts festivals needs to have equal weight in funding and policy decisions, along with the other factors being considered. This is the main way to increase participation in, rather than consumption or exploitation of, the arts (Putnam, 2001).

References

Bailey, C., Miles, S. and Stark, P. (2004) 'Culture-led urban regeneration and the revitalisation of identities in Newcastle, Gateshead and the North East of England', *International Journal of Cultural Policy*, Vol. 10, No. 1: pp. 47–65.

Barrow, C. (2000) *Social impact assessment: An introduction*. London: Arnold Publishers.

Belfiore. E. (2006) 'The social impacts of the arts — myth or reality?', in Mirza, M. (ed) *Culture vultures: Is UK arts policy damaging the arts?*. London: Policy Exchange, pp. 20–37.

Brighton, A. (2006) 'Consumed by the political: The ruination of the Arts Council', in Mirza, M. (ed) *Culture vultures: Is UK arts policy damaging the arts?*. London: Policy Exchange, pp. 111–129.

Burdge, R. (1999) *A community guide to social impact assessment* (Rev. ed.). Wisconsin: Social Ecology Press.

Dayton-Johnson, J. and King, E. (2003) *Subsidising Stan: Measuring the social benefits of cultural spending*. Halifax: Department of Canadian Heritage.

Department for Culture, Media and Sport (1998) *A new cultural framework*. London: DCMS.

Ekman, A.K. (1999) 'The revival of cultural celebrations in regional Sweden: Aspects of tradition and transition', *Sociologia Ruralis*, Vol. 39, No. 3: pp. 280–293.

Finsterbusch, K., Llewellyn, L. and Wolf, C. (1983) *Social impact assessment methods*. New York: Sage Publications.

Fredline, E., Jago, L., Deery, M. (2004) 'Triple bottom line evaluation: Progress toward a technique to assist in planning and managing an event in a sustainable manner', paper presented at Tourism: State of the Art II International Scientific Conference, University of Strathclyde, Glasgow.

Gibson, C. and Klocker, N. (2005) 'The 'cultural turn' in Australian regional economic development discourse: Neoliberalising creativity?', *Geographical Research*, Vol. 43, No. 1: pp. 93–102.

Gray, C. (2000) *The politics of the arts in Britain*. London: Macmillan Press Ltd.

Hewison, R. (1994) 'Public policy: Corporate culture: Public culture', in O. Robinson, R. Freeman, C. Riley II (eds) *The arts in the world economy: Public policy and private philanthropy for a global cultural community* (Salzburg seminar). London: University Press of New England, pp. 26–32.

Laird, K. (2003) personal interview.

Lehrer, B. (2004) 'Make the street fair less generic', *The New York Times*, 4 January.

Mirza, M. (ed) (2006) *Culture vultures: Is UK arts policy damaging the arts?*. London: Policy Exchange.

Muir, E. (1997) *Ritual in early modern Europe*. Cambridge: Cambridge University Press.

Myerscough, J. and Bruce, A. (1988) *The economic importance of the arts in Britain*. London: Policy Studies Institute. National Economics (2004) 'State of Regions' report: www.nieir.com.au/about_us/company.asp.

Putnam, R. (2001) *Bowling alone: The collapse and revival of American community*. New York: Simon & Schuster.

Quinn, B. (2005) 'Arts festivals and the city', *Urban Studies*, Vol. 42, No. 5/6: pp. 927–943.

Riding, A. (2005) 'British arts: rich in funds, but still a poor cousin', *The New York Times*, 28 April: pp. E9.

Rolfe, H. (1992) *Arts festivals in the UK*. London: Policy Studies Institute.

Selwood, S. (2006) 'Unreliable evidence: The rhetorics of data collection in the cultural sector', in Mirza, M. (ed) *Culture vultures: Is UK arts policy damaging the arts?*. London: Policy Exchange, pp. 38–52.

Sherwood, P., Jago, L. and Deery, M. (2005) 'Triple bottom line evaluation of special events: Does the rhetoric reflect reporting?', paper presented to Annual Council of Australian Tourism and Hospitality Educators' Conference, Alice Springs.

Small, K., Edwards, D. and Sheridan, L. (2005) 'A flexible framework for evaluating the socio-cultural impacts of a (small) festival', *International Journal of Event Management Research*, Vol. 1, No. 1: pp. 66–77.

Smith, S. (1993) 'Bounding the borders: Claiming space and making place in rural Scotland', *Transactions of the Institute of British Geographers*, Vol. 18, No. 3: pp. 291–309.

Stevens, D. (2004) Personal interview.

Turner, V. (1982) *Celebration: Studies in festivity and ritual*. Washington, DC: Smithsonian Institution Press.

Wildman, P. and Baker, G. (1985) *Social impacts assessment handbook: How to assess and evaluate the social impact of resource development on local communities*. Lindfield, Australia: Social Impacts Publications.

Leisure Studies Association

LSA Publications

LSA

An extensive list of publications on a wide range of leisure studies topics, produced by the Leisure Studies Association since the late 1970s, is available from LSA Publications.

Some of the more recently published volumes are detailed on the following pages, and full information may be obtained on newer and forthcoming LSA volumes from:

LSA Publications, c/o M. McFee
email: mcfee@solutions-inc.co.uk
The Chelsea School, University of Brighton
Eastbourne BN20 7SP (UK)

Among other benefits, members of the Leisure Studies Association may purchase LSA Publications at preferential rates. Please contact LSA at the above address for information regarding membership of the Association, LSA Conferences, and LSA Newsletters.

ONLINE

Complete information about LSA Publications:

www.leisure-studies-association.info/LSAWEB/Publications.html

EVALUATING SPORT AND ACTIVE LEISURE FOR YOUNG PEOPLE

**LSA Publication No. 88.   ISBN: 0 906337 99 2 [2005] pp. 236+xviii
eds. Kevyn Hylton, Anne Flintoff and Jonathan Long**

Contents

LSA Publication No. 88. (cont.)

YOUTH SPORT AND ACTIVE LEISURE: THEORY, POLICY AND PARTICIPATION

LSA Publication No. 87.   ISBN: 0 906337 98 4 [2005] pp. 185 + xii eds. Anne Flintoff, Jonathan Long and Kevyn Hylton

Contents

SPORT AND ACTIVE LEISURE YOUTH CULTURES

**LSA PUBLICATIONS NO. 86. ISBN: 0 906337 97 6 [2005] pp. 238 + xxii
eds. Jayne Caudwell and Peter Bramham**

Contents

LEISURE, SPACE AND VISUAL CULTURE: PRACTICES AND MEANINGS

LSA Publication No. 84. ISBN: 0 906337 95 X [2004] pp. 292+xxii
eds. Cara Aitchison and Helen Pussard

Contents

LEISURE, MEDIA AND VISUAL CULTURE: REPRESENTATIONS AND CONTESTATIONS

LSA Publication No. 83. ISBN: 0 906337 94 1 [2004] pp. 282
eds. Eileen Kennedy and Andrew Thornton

Contents

SPORT, LEISURE AND SOCIAL INCLUSION

LSA Publication No. 82. ISBN: 0 906337 933 [2003] pp. 296
ed. Adrian Ibbetseon, Beccy Watson and Maggie Ferguson

Contents

ACCESS AND INCLUSION IN LEISURE AND TOURISM

LSA Publication No. 81. ISBN: 0 906337 92 5 [2003] pp. 288
eds. Bob Snape, Edwin Thwaites, Christine Williams

Contents

VOLUNTEERS IN SPORT

**LSA Publication No. 80. ISBN: 0 906337 91 7 [2003] pp. 107
ed. Geoff Nichols**

Contents

LEISURE CULTURES: INVESTIGATIONS IN SPORT, MEDIA AND TECHNOLOGY

LSA Publication No. 79. ISBN: 0 906337 90 9 [2003] pp. 221 + xii
Eds. Scott Fleming and Ian Jones

Contents

PARTNERSHIPS IN LEISURE: SPORT, TOURISM AND MANAGEMENT

**LSA Publication No. 78. ISBN: 0 906337 89 5 [2002] pp. 245 + iv
eds. Graham Berridge and Graham McFee**

Contents

LEISURE STUDIES:
TRENDS IN THEORY AND RESEARCH

**LSA Publication No. 77. ISBN: 0 906337 88 7 [2001] pp. 198 + iv
eds. Stan Parker and Lesley Lawrence**

Contents

SPORT TOURISM: PRINCIPLES AND PRACTICE

LSA Publication No. 76. ISBN: 0 906337 87 9 [2001] pp. 174 + xii
eds. Sean Gammin and Joseph Kurtzman

Contents

VOLUNTEERING IN LEISURE: MARGINAL OR INCLUSIVE?

**LSA Publication No. 75. ISBN: 0 906337 86 0 [2001] pp. 158+xi
eds. Margaret Graham and Malcolm Foley**

Contents

LEISURE CULTURES, CONSUMPTION AND COMMODIFICATION

LSA Publication No. 74. ISBN: 0 906337 85 2 [2001] pp. 158+xi
ed. John Horne

Contents

LEISURE AND SOCIAL INCLUSION: NEW CHALLENGES FOR POLICY AND PROVISION

LSA Publication No. 73. ISBN: 0 906337 84 4 [2001] pp. 204
eds. Gayle McPherson and Malcolm Reid

Contents

JUST LEISURE:
EQUITY, SOCIAL EXCLUSION AND IDENTITY

**LSA Publication No 72. ISBN: 0 906337 83 6 [2000] pp. 195+xiv
Edited by Celia Brackenridge, David Howe and Fiona Jordan**

Contents

JUST LEISURE:
POLICY, ETHICS & PROFESSIONALISM

LSA Publication No 71. ISBN: 0 906337 81 X [2000] pp. 257+xiv
Edited by Celia Brackenridge, David Howe and Fiona Jordan

Contents

WOMEN'S LEISURE EXPERIENCES: AGES, STAGES AND ROLES

LSA Publication No. 70. ISBN 0 906337 80 1 [2001]
Edited by Sharon Clough and Judy White

Contents

MASCULINITIES: LEISURE CULTURES, IDENTITIES AND CONSUMPTION

LSA Publication No. 69. ISBN: 0 906337 77 1 [2000] pp. 163

Edited by John Horne and Scott Fleming

Contents

GENDER ISSUES IN WORK AND LEISURE

LSA Publication No. 68.ISBN 0 906337 78 X [2000]
Edited by Jenny Anderson and Lesley Lawrence [pp. 173]

Contents

SPORT, LEISURE IDENTITIES AND GENDERED SPACES

LSA Publication No. 67. ISBN: 0 906337 79 8 [1999] pp. 196
Edited by Sheila Scraton and Becky Watson

Contents

HER OUTDOORS: RISK, CHALLENGE AND ADVENTURE IN GENDERED OPEN SPACES

LSA Publication No. 66 [1999] ISBN: 0 906337 76 3; pp. 131
Edited by Barbara Humberstone

Contents

POLICY AND PUBLICS

LSA Publication No. 65. ISBN: 0 906337 75 5 [1999] pp. 167
Edited by Peter Bramham and Wilf Murphy

Contents

CONSUMPTION AND PARTICIPATION: LEISURE, CULTURE AND COMMERCE

LSA Publication No. 64. ISBN: 0 906337 74 7 [2000]
Edited by Garry Whannel

Contents

GENDER, SPACE AND IDENTITY: LEISURE, CULTURE AND COMMERCE

LSA Publication No. 63. ISBN: 0 906337 73 9 [1998] pp. 191
Edited by Cara Aitchison and Fiona Jordan

Contents

THE PRODUCTION AND CONSUMPTION OF SPORT CULTURES: LEISURE, CULTURE AND COMMERCE

LSA Publication No. 62. ISBN: 0 906337 72 0 [1998] pp. 178
Edited by Udo Merkel, Gill Lines, Ian McDonald

Contents

TOURISM AND VISITOR ATTRACTIONS: LEISURE, CULTURE AND COMMERCE

LSA Publication No 61. ISBN: 0 906337 71 2 [1998] pp. 211
Edited by Neil Ravenscroft, Deborah Philips and Marion Bennett

Contents

LEISURE PLANNING IN TRANSITORY SOCIETIES

LSA Publication No. 58. ISBN: 0 906337 70 4
Edited by Mike Collins; pp 218

Contents

LEISURE, TIME AND SPACE: MEANINGS AND VALUES IN PEOPLE'S LIVES

LSA Publication No. 57. ISBN: 0 906337 68 2 [1998] pp. 198 + IV
Edited by Sheila Scraton

Contents

LEISURE, TOURISM AND ENVIRONMENT (I) SUSTAINABILITY AND ENVIRONMENTAL POLICIES

LSA Publication No. 50 Part I; ISBN 0 906337 64 X
Edited by Malcolm Foley, David McGillivray and Gayle McPherson (1999);

Contents

LEISURE, TOURISM AND ENVIRONMENT (II) PARTICIPATION, PERCEPTIONS AND PREFERENCES

**LSA Publication No. 50 (Part II) ISBN: 0 906337 69 0; pp. 177+xii
Edited by Malcolm Foley, Matt Frew and Gayle McPherson**

Contents

LEISURE: MODERNITY, POSTMODERNITY AND LIFESTYLES

LSA Publications No. 48 (LEISURE IN DIFFERENT WORLDS Volume I)
Edited by Ian Henry (1994); ISBN: 0 906337 52 6, pp. 375+

Contents

LSA Publications No. 48 (cont.)